THE SPLENDOUR OF DOCTRINE

THE SPLENDOUR OF DOCTRINE

The *Catechism of the Catholic Church* on Christian Believing

Aidan Nichols, O.P.

WIPF & STOCK · Eugene, Oregon

Wipf and Stock Publishers
199 W 8th Ave, Suite 3
Eugene, OR 97401

The Splendour of Doctrine
The 'Catechism of the Catholic Church' on Christian Believing
By Nichols, Aidan, OP
Copyright©1995 The Dominican Council
ISBN 13: 978-1-61097-843-9
Publication date 12/1/2011
Previously published by T & T Clark, 1995

Lord God,
since by the adoption of grace,
you have made us children of light:
do not let false doctrine darken our minds,
but grant that your light may shine within us
and we may always live in the brightness of truth.

Oratio of the Roman rite for the
Thirteenth Sunday of the Year

Contents

Preface		ix
I.	Transmitting the Faith: The Pope's Introduction	1
II.	Alerting the Reader: The Authors' Prologue	9
III.	Professing the Faith: The Creed and Revelation	17
IV.	Professing the Faith: The Creed on the Father	33
V.	Professing the Faith: The Creed on the Son	51
VI.	Professing the Faith: The Creed on the Holy Spirit	99
Index		161

Preface

The word 'catholic' comes from a Greek phrase which, if we translated it literally, would mean 'according to the whole', or, as we say in modern English, 'holistic'. In other words, the Church is catholic not only because she is called to preach to, and be present among, all peoples (quantitative catholicity). She is catholic also because she has a holistic or all-round grasp of God's revelation in Jesus Christ (qualitative catholicity). The Word made flesh told his disciples that the Paraclete, the Holy Spirit, would 'lead them into all the truth', and so the Church never lacks the ability to present divine revelation in an overall way, a well-rounded way, with its great contours intact.

This matters to us – for two reasons. First, we want to know that our faith is 'the truth, the whole truth, and nothing but the truth'. And second, only the whole faith can answer to the needs of the whole human being. The Fathers of the Church used to say that Christ must be fully man, for, if he had not assumed the whole of human nature, the whole man (ourselves) would not be saved. And similarly, unless the Church can give us the whole of God's truth about ourselves, the whole of God's plan for us, we cannot reach the wholeness – the happiness and holiness – for which we were made, and into which we were redeemed.

Hence the Church's concern, in the *Catechism*, to hold all the splendours of the faith before us so that we can see the Catholic tradition, and the Christian life, for what they are – a seamless web of beauty, truth and goodness which reflects, ultimately, the very being of God himself. The whole faith means, first and foremost, the whole Creed, the whole confession of Catholic doctrine. In the Church's doctrinal teaching, particular truths dovetail together in a harmony which we spoil if we attempt to pick and choose among them. It has well been said that the unity of doctrine is like a face:

change one feature, and the whole looks different. What the *Catechism* has to say about the Creed is the foundation for the rest of its teaching – on the sacraments, the moral life, prayer and spirituality. I have, therefore, dealt with it at considerably greater length than with the remaining sections of the work; hence its publication as the first part of a diptych: the *Catechism* on *belief*, the *Catechism* on *practice*.

The Letter of James reminds us that faith without works is hardly alive. The 'works' which the *Catechism* will go on to describe are essentially threefold: sacramental, ethical, spiritual. For, once again: the whole faith means the whole sacramental life of the Church. The sacraments mediate life in Christ, and they do so by taking up into the sphere of the Redeemer all that is really essential in our life here below. The whole faith means, too, the whole of the ethos, or moral living, of the Catholic Church. Finally, the whole faith means the whole of spirituality, the whole of that conscious relationship with Father, Son and Holy Spirit, and the redeemed city of the angels and saints, which we call the life of prayer. After expounding what the *Catechism* has to say on these vital topics, I will go on, in the sequel to the present study, to investigate and respond to some of the criticisms that have been voiced of the *Catechism's* project, and/or the way in which it has been effected. Some words on the artworks used to illustrate the French paradigm of the *Catechism*, and a select bibliography, will close this second book.

Although both parts of this study may be read intelligibly in their own right, they are obviously intended to be used side by side with the *Catechism* itself. For this reason, I have avoided copious quotation; such direct citations as do appear are taken from the official English translation. The Holy Scriptures are quoted in the Revised Standard Version, Catholic edition.

I must thank Geoffrey Green and Stratford Caldecott of T&T Clark for suggesting that I write this study, and the latter for providing me with the essay series on themes in the *Catechism* from *L'Osservatore Romano*.

Blackfriars, Cambridge
Feast of St John Fisher and St Thomas More, 1994

I

Transmitting the Faith: The Pope's Introduction

Pope John Paul II, in introducing the *Catechism of the Catholic Church* and commending it to those for whom it was written, took pains to relate this new text to an event which he evidently saw as its fountain-head: the Second Vatican Council. In the twenty-five years which separate that Council from the promulgation of the *Catechism*, a variety of views about 'Vatican II' have surfaced and found both supporters and critics. Some interpretations were manifestly abusive; others shared legitimacy among them, for in the Council's rich corpus of doctrine were many themes each of which might be singled out as the sun of its planets. The pope himself uses a metaphor of *light* to present the special contribution of the Council to modern Catholicism in terms of *theological aesthetics*. Its aim was to show up the *beauty* of Catholic faith and life.

Thus he speaks of the Council as intended to 'illuminate the apostolic and pastoral mission of the Church'; by 'making the truth of the Gospel shine forth', the Conciliar Fathers would lead all human beings to seek out and welcome in their lives the love of Christ which surpasses all knowledge – a reference to the Letter to the Ephesians with its masterly orchestration of the themes of the glory of God, lavishing rich grace through the beloved Son on the Church which is his 'fullness', her members 'light in the Lord'.[1] The task which the initiator of the Council – Pope John XXIII – had given it was the 'better

---

[1] *Fidei depositum*, 1.

keeping and presentation' (note the duality of moments, one preservative, the other communicative) 'of the precious deposit of Christian doctrine', making that treasure-hoard more accessible both to the faithful and to human beings at large. The Council, Pope John Paul continues, was not intended to condemn the errors of our epoch – but he does not draw from this historical fact the conclusion that the Council was not therefore concerned with the setting forth of doctrine but only with some (vaguely conceived) benevolent exhortation to the men and women of our time. The pope takes this misconception – found, as a compliment, on the Catholic Left, as an insult on the Catholic Right – and stands it on its head. *The very absence of dogmatic anathemas at Vatican II testifies to the thorough-goingly doctrinal character of its conception and execution.* For, had it concentrated on a few, probably negative, dogmatic disputed questions, it would not have succeeded in its task, which was to furnish a doctrinal overview of Catholic teaching in its total harmony. Its agenda, read at the deepest level, consisted in 'demonstrating in serene fashion, the power and beauty of the teaching of the faith'.[2]

The work of renovating the Church, begun by the Council, must be considered, then, as a more effective disclosure of the force, radiance and inspirational power of Christian truth in its plenary Catholic form – rather than as the execution of a particular reformist agenda. Naturally, such a goal would be nebulous idealism unless it were translated into concrete directives for each aspect of the Church's life – and this the pope claims as the occupation and achievement of his pontificate. It was at the 1985 'Extraordinary Synod' of the world episcopate, summoned to evaluate the fruits of the Council that the notion of producing a 'universal Catechism' was formally accepted. The Council's own doctrinal project was now to be expressed in a 'compendium' of Catholic teaching in its totality, in matters both of faith and of morals, with the practical aim of providing a 'reference point' for the catechetical manuals of particular churches, or groups of churches, in different parts of the world. Like the Council

[2] Ibid., 1.

itself, the *Catechism* would be typified by a process of *ressourcement*, going back to the sources. It would present doctrine in a fashion inspired by Scripture and liturgies of the Church. At the same time, it would not lack a sense of pastoral actuality, once again mirroring the Council: the text would be 'adapted to the present life of Christians'.³ To these articulations of the desirable coming from the floor of the house, the bishops in synod, the pope had added his own voice. Such a Catechism would meet a real need in the Church universal and the particular churches: doubtless he was quite aware, through the regular *ad limina* visits of bishops to Rome, the organs of the Roman Curia, and his own global journeyings, of the doctrinal confusion, ignorance or at least vagueness which afflicted much post-Conciliar Catholicism in many places.

Certainly there was no lack of consultation, and laborious re-editing, of the resultant text. Episcopal Conferences (national bodies of bishops) in the Western church, synods in the Eastern, had been invited to comment, as had the members of institutes of Catholic theology and catechesis. No less than nine drafts had succeeded one another before an episcopal committee had proved able to satisfy a commission of twelve cardinals and bishops, presided over by the prefect of the Congregation for the Doctrine of the Faith, Cardinal Joseph Ratzinger. It is a name which inspires confidence in those who care for the integrity of Christian doctrine, and, at the same time, wish to see that doctrine expounded with humanity and historical and spiritual richness of reference. The final synthesis, so the pope believes, reflects the 'symphony' of the faith – many instruments playing in unison, a favoured metaphor both of Ratzinger and of the Swiss cardinal theologian, much admired by Pope John Paul II, Hans Urs von Balthasar.⁴ It

---

³Extraordinary Synod of Bishops, *Final Report* II B.a.4; *Synod Report. The Final Report and Message to the People of God of the Extraordinary General Assembly of the Synod of Bishops Rome, 24 November – 8 December 1985, on the Theme: The Second Vatican Council. A Celebration, Re-affirmation and Carrying Forward of its Work* (E.t. London 1986).

⁴See my *The Theology of Joseph Ratzinger. An Introductory Study* (Edinburgh 1988), pp. 284–291; also H. U. von Balthasar, *Truth is Symphonic. Aspects of Christian Pluralism* (E.t. San Francisco 1987).

chimes with the collegial nature of the episcopate: solidary, yet dispersed in a multitude of churches throughout the world. It also testifies to the catholicity of the Church: though manifold, she is one.

The pope now turns to consider what his introductory statement calls, somewhat banally, 'the distribution of the matter'.[5] In fact what follows is a brilliant exercise in the compressed statement of the *Catechism's* own working principles. First, the pope considers the content the *Catechism* proposes to convey. That content is nothing less than that of the sources of revelation themselves, as they are scanned by various aids to discernment which Catholic divinity has made its own. Faithfully and organically, that is, with accuracy and a concern for the internal coherence of the whole, the *Catechism* will re-present in a new medium the content of Scripture, Tradition and the teaching put forth by the Church's magisterium, while also bringing into play the witness of the Fathers and the saints of the Church. The spiritual patrimony of the Fathers and of the holy men and women of the Church will help readers to penetrate the depths of the Christian mystery and inflame the smouldering embers of faith among the people of God. This appeal to the Fathers as granting privileged access to the meaning of revelation is traditional in Catholic exegesis and spirituality. The Fathers were massive presences at the Second Vatican Council, and the Missal and Liturgy of the Hours commissioned by Pope Paul VI in the Council's wake form a mosaic of fragments from their writings. They have been, unfortunately, less apparent in much post-Conciliar theology. The Holy See has rightly drawn attention, in the recent past, to their continuing, because perennial, significance.[6] Reference to the lives and writings of the saints is less expected, yet it is a staple of Catholic piety, and a most important expression, therefore, of the 'sense of the faithful'. Both appeal to the Fathers of the early centuries and reference

---

[5]*Depositum fidei*, 3.
[6]E.g. Congregation for Catholic Education, *Instruction on the Study of the Fathers of the Church in the Formation of Priests* (Rome 1989).

to the spiritual fatherhood and motherhood exercised by the saints in all the ages, will render the *Catechism* sympathetic to Eastern Catholics, and indeed to their separated brethren, the Eastern Orthodox.

Two riders are now mentioned. A Catholic catechism will naturally want to take into account doctrinal development whereby what was originally tacit in the apostolic Writings and the apostolic Tradition has become explicit in the post-apostolic age. And with the lead given by the Holy See in addressing, through encyclicals of the popes and declarations by dicasteries (curial departments), a vast range of contemporary problems from the structure of international trade to *in vitro* fertilisation, a catechism promulgated by Roman authority will not wish to be behind hand in indicating orientations of thought and practice for new situations, unknown to the past of Tradition. In sum, the *Catechism*, like the treasure-house of the 'scribe of the Kingdom' in St Matthew's Gospel, will contain both old things and new – quite appropriate for a faith which is, as the pope remarks, 'always the same and yet a source of ever new light'.[7]

And this *nova et vetera* approach suggests the procedure the *Catechism* will adopt in unfolding its own content. On the one hand, it would not wish to leave behind the time-hallowed format (early canonised in the *Roman Catechism* issued by the Dominican Pope Pius V) of a book in four parts (the Creed, the sacraments, the Commandments, the Our Father). On the other hand, it would hope to fill this venerable structure with materials presented in a novel way.

And here we come to the master-stroke in the pope's preamble, which is the way the four sections (on dogmatic believing, worship, Christian action, and prayer) are interrelated. The key concept used to bring off this *coup* is that of the 'Christian mystery'. First and foremost that means the God of creation and salvation in his self-revelation, both general (in nature) and specific (in history), as the divine Persons reach out through the humanity of Christ and his Church to human persons, namely ourselves. This is a supremely *objective* reality,

---

[7] *Depositum fidei*, 3.

but one of an *inter-subjective* kind. But secondly, the phrase 'the Christian mystery' also denotes the Church's registering of that wondrous self-gift of the Holy Trinity, as revelation is impressed on her corporate, Spirit-illumined, mind. Here we are dealing with a *subjective* reality, but one of a *uniquely veridical* kind: the saving truth, the whole saving truth, and nothing but the saving truth. This Christian mystery, then, is, the pope explains, treated initially in the *Catechism* as the *object of faith*. That is what the first sub-book, on the Creed, takes for its topic. But the same mystery which is faith's object is also something celebrated and communicated – and this happens in the *liturgical life*, to which the *Catechism's* second sub-book, on the sacraments, is devoted. But thirdly, the Christian mystery is 'present to illuminate and sustain the children of God in their action', the *ethical agenda* appropriate to the new life of the Kingdom. And so the third section of the *Catechism* takes as its theme Christian morality, whose various dimensions are conveniently signalled by the Ten Commandments. Then lastly, 'the Christian mystery' may be said to 'found' our prayer, and – evidently in what I have called the primary, objective but inter-subjective, acceptation of that phrase – 'constitutes the object of our supplication, praise and intercession'. This final modality of the mystery in its impact on human lives provides the subject matter of the *Catechism's* closing section, on *spirituality and prayer*, with, as its climax, a commentary on the *Lord's Prayer*, the model of all praying.

Before abandoning the topic of the inter-relations found in the *Catechism* text, the pope points out for good measure some further connexions. Because the faith is solemnly confessed in the Liturgy (especially in the recitation of the Creed); because the Liturgy is itself prayer; and because, finally, sacramental grace – the way God's gift of his life is attuned to human need through the various sacraments – is a necessary condition of Christian living, no one could gain a just idea of the *Catechism's* vision of any one of its four chosen topics without looking at how it handles the other three.

And in a closing theological comment, Pope John Paul underlines two theological themes of constitutive importance for any such compendium of doctrine: the marvellous *unity* of

God's saving design, and the *centrality* within that design of the figure of Christ. A unified Christocentric scheme of salvation will be the *Catechism's* most obvious feature. The mystery of the Saviour forms the living, personal unity of the *Catechism's* four parts: for he is the source of faith, the saving presence in the sacraments, the model of Christian action and the master of Christian prayer.

The pope signs off by describing the *Catechism* as a work of reference, at once reliable and authoritative, for all those who need to know their Catholic doctrine as teachers and learners. It will serve ecclesial communion not least because the unity of faith and faithfulness to Catholic doctrine are conditions of the flourishing of that communion. Though local catechisms edited in the light of the great *Catechism* are necessary for the better adaptation of catechesis to particular cultures, their writing must not be at the expense of these primordial values. Otherwise the *Catechism of the Catholic Church* would simply re-launch the churches in communion with Rome on the high seas of relativism, where their last state might be worse than their first. Certainly, it will be crucial for the future to ensure that the regional or local 'adaptation' of the *Catechism* concerns style rather than content. The bottom line must be that all new catechisms incorporate the full range of doctrinal propositions put forward in the great *Catechism*, diverging from it only in the choice of texts, episodes and examples used to illustrate its truths.

In conclusion, it is worth nothing the four biblical texts with which the pope rounds off his commendation of the book. In Luke 22:32 Christ, on his way to his Passion, promises St Peter that when he has 'turned again' (after his lapse into betrayal), he will 'strengthen' or 'confirm' his brethren – one of the Gospel texts regarded by Catholicism as evidence for the Petrine primacy. Pope John Paul sees the *Catechism* as an instance of such attempted strengthening. A fuller and clearer view of the common doctrine of the Church can only reinforce the bonds of apostolic faith which join the churches of the *Catholica* one to another. In John 8:32, Jesus tells his Jewish sympathisers that, if they continue to accept his teaching, they will know the truth and the truth will set them free. It is because saving truth provides definitive liberation that it is of burning existential concern: freedom from error and from the slavery from sin are the two principal kinds of negative liberty which lead on to the only positive liberty fully worthy of that name. It is by reference to this text from St John that the pope identifies the service the *Catechism* can offer to all the faithful (and not just the bishops) on the one hand, and, on the other, to the cause of Christian unity. What could be more useful to ecumenism, *correctly understood*, than an exact portrayal of the content and harmonious coherence of the Catholic faith?[8] I Peter 3:15 is the historic charter of apologetics; in it, St Peter bids his correspondents 'always [to] be prepared to make a defence to any one who calls you to account for the hope that is in you'. But the pope expands the ambit of his apostolic predecessor's words by underlining how enquirers may want to know not just the rational evidences for Catholic Christianity but the whole of what the Catholic Church believes. Lastly, in I Corinthians 13:13 and II Corinthians 5:6–8, St Paul points to the final destiny of the Church: the *patria* of heaven, where we shall understand as fully as we are understood, and see God face to face. The pope thus marks out for the *Catechism* a lowly yet merited place on the journey by which the light of faith becomes effulgent in glory.

---

[8]Frère Max Thurian remarks in this connexion that, in ecumenical dialogue, 'the lack was often felt of a reference text in which one could find the full, unequivocal teaching of the Catholic Church in all its homogeneous development, including the important stage of Vatican II', 'Reflections on the *Catechism of the Catholic Church* – 6', *L'Osservatore Romano*, 7 April 1993, p. 4.

II

*Alerting the Reader: The Authors' Prologue**

Before plunging *in medias res* the editors of the *Catechism* have paused to offer their own general orientation to the reader of the book. Since their Prologue both confirms our interpretation of the pope's introductory letter and adds some refinements, notably in the way of practical tips, it is worth delaying for a moment to take it in.

The Prologue does not begin from an anthropological starting-point. It does not take its rise from investigation – whether sociological or more personal – of the human 'problem', nor does it situate itself in the midst of human religious experience at large. Its point of departure is unashamedly theological. It begins with God; his plan; the divine agency in that plan's execution, the Son, Jesus Christ, and the Holy Spirit. Only because the God of all perfection out of sheer goodness wished his human creatures to share in some way his own blissfully happy life does catechesis – the making and using of catechisms – exist at all. For the outcome of the divine philanthropy was that, to gather a sinful race into the unity of his family, God sent his Son as man's Redeemer. Through his Son, the Father calls all human beings to become, in the Holy Spirit, his adopted children, and so heirs to a patrimony: the blessed life which the Father has communicated from all eternity to the Son, the life Father and Son have

---

* = *Catechism*, Paragraphs 1–25.

exulted over in the Holy Spirit, and which is now extended, as a gift, to the rational creation.

The key-word here is *mission*. The eternal procession of the Son, and of the Spirit, archetypal 'events' within the divine life, are prolonged in the missions of the same Son and Spirit to the world of space and time. Here the unseen God works as Redeemer and Sanctifier to change the conditions on which the world, and humanity within it, has its existence – just as once, as Creator, he constituted their original terms of being in the first place. But this divine initiative, addressed as it is to the minds and hearts of free creatures, must continue to be as humanly intelligible as it was when the Word made flesh, Jesus Christ, spoke human language on earth. In order that this call, then, might resound through all the earth, Christ mandated his chosen apostles to preach his Gospel to all nations: here the Prologue cites the Great Commission given by the risen Christ at the end of St Matthew's Gospel (28:19–20). And paralleling those closing words of the First Gospel, stand their equivalent in the Second, where St Mark reports that the apostles did as they were bidden, the Lord assisting them and confirming their word by 'signs' – what the later Church has called *signs of credibility* whereby the world-transforming power of the Gospel is manifested in the lives of believers. This apostolic mission continues in the apostolic Church: indeed, the Church is apostolic precisely through sharing this mission, the outward mark of whose continuity is the apostolic succession of her ordained ministry, with its passing on of a charge, through the laying on of hands, from the generation of the apostles to our own. Although the Prologue refers without embarrassment to the 'treasure received from the apostles'[1] – the integral truth of divine revelation in Christ – as the object of a conservative, one might even say, *conservationist*, task of keeping and guarding on the part of the apostles' successors, the entire context makes it clear that such defensive protectionism – the defence of orthodoxy – is in the service of the expansive and forward policy of spreading the Good News throughout the earth. After

---

[1] *Prologue*, 3.

all, in the adage of the mediaeval spiritual theologians, *Nemo dat quod non habet*: 'no one can give what they have not got'.
Not that such giving is restricted to the episcopate. All the baptised should echo St Paul's cry, 'Woe to me if I preach not the Gospel' (I Corinthians 9:16). So all of Christ's faithful – namely, all the members of the Catholic Church, the term here is a technical one, *Christifideles* – have the duty to transmit the Gospel, something they can do, the Prologue remarks, in the four ways that correspond to the *Catechism*'s four parts: by proclaiming their faith in words (part one), by living it in 'fraternal sharing'[2] (part three), by celebrating it in the Liturgy and prayer (parts two and four). And the mission of the entire Church to spread the Catholic faith (explicitly or implicitly, or, best of all, by both means together) takes as its inspired mottoes the three biblical texts which stand as preface to the Prologue of the *Catechism* as a whole. The God-centred and Christ-centred character of their (spoken or silent) message comes over well in the first text the authors have chosen (the opening text, then, of the *entire Catechism*): 'This is eternal life, that they know thee, the only true God, and Jesus Christ, whom thou hast sent' (John 17:3). (Those were the words, incidentally, at which the New Testament fell open, at St John Fisher's execution, and which that proto-martyr of the English Reformation described as 'learning enough to last [him] even to [his] life's end'.[3]) The remaining two texts speak of the universal character of God's saving will, which extends to each and every human being, and of the essential rôle of the human intelligence and human understanding in this project, for God our Saviour 'desires all men to be saved and to come to the knowledge of the truth' (I Timothy 2:3–4), as also of the indispensable mediation of Jesus Christ in the whole work of salvation: 'For of all the names in the world given to men, this is the only one by which we can be saved' (Acts 4:12).

Given that the mission to pass on the faith, in which mission the *Catechism* has its home, is ordered to making known humanity's definitive fulfilment, and even *super*-fulfilment, in

[2]Ibid.
[3]As recorded in William Rastell's *Certain Brief Notes appertaining to Bishop Fisher*; see E. E. Reynolds, *Saint John Fisher* (London 1955), p. 283.

God (for sharing the life of communion of Father, Son and Holy Spirit, is a gift which exceeds all our nature could ask), it will not surprise us that the authors treat catechesis as an introduction to the Christian life in its fullness. It is not merely elementary instruction; it is meant to be an initiation into the new life of grace within the covenant community of Christ's Church, and, on that basis, an empowerment to be truly apostolic. Those who have never felt the converting force of missionary preaching; or mastered the chief arguments and evidences for Christian truth in apologetics, or had experience of the Christian life in depth, or celebrated the sacraments according to the mind of the Church, or committed themselves with heart and soul to Catholicism (what the Prologue calls 'integration into the ecclesial community'[4]), will not be cogent spokespersons for the Gospel in its plenary form, and this is true whether they be bishops, priests, deacons, or layfolk. So catechesis must take as its object the evangelical animation of all these elements. In themselves they are not the same as catechesis; but good catechesis is their soul, just as, reciprocally, the ability to inspire them from within is the test of good catechesis. Not surprisingly, the Prologue identifies the outstanding periods of history for catechesis as the blossom-times of the Church herself: notably, the patristic age, and the Catholic Reformation of the sixteenth century. The effort at Church renewal made at the Second Vatican Council had inevitably, then, a catechetical dimension. But its harvest, in the 1971 *General Catechetical Directory* and the apostolic exhortations *Evangelii nuntiandi* (1975), and *Catechesi tradendae* (1979), following on episcopal synods dedicated respectively to evangelisation and catechetics, might be considered, in the light of these earlier models, rather meagre. Hence no doubt the eagerness with which the Holy See set to work on the present *Catechism* once it had established the consent of the episcopate to the general idea in 1985.

The authors of the Prologue feel bold enough to make some high claims for the *Catechism* that has thus appeared. It is, they say, an organic or synthetic presentation of essentials or

---

[4]*Prologue*, 6.

fundamentals, both of faith and morals. In other words, they lay most weight, in the *Catechism's* making, on two features: the internal inter-relatedness of the whole, and its 'back to basics' quality. They concur with the pope's estimate of the *Catechism's* chief sources when they describe these as, in order, the Scriptures, the Fathers, the Liturgy and the magisterium of the Church: and indeed even a casual perusal of the text's references would ascertain the well-foundedness of this claim. The Prologue gives slightly more emphasis than the pope to the bishops as the primary recipients of the *Catechism*, speaking of its utilisation by priests and catechists as taking place 'through' the episcopate, while the ordinary faithful are told, somewhat glacially, that they may find the book 'useful reading'.[5] Here the pope surely shows a better grasp of ecclesial (and even publishing) realities.

The Prologue's analysis of the four parts of the *Catechism* is rather more wooden than the pope's – but it is also more informative. It describes the four 'pillars' by summarising formulaically the content of each part, and so gives the user a helpful orientation for their reading. In Part One, the *Catechism* addresses the main task of all Christian instruction, enabling the baptised to carry out their principal duty which is the confessing of baptismal faith before men. Here we consider what *is* this 'revelation' whereby God speaks to man, and this 'faith' whereby humanity replies to God. Having considered what, in grand outline, revelation and its correlate, faith, may be, the *Catechism* describes their content by reproducing the Trinitarian structure of the Creed. It sums up the gifts of God as Author of all good, as Redeemer, and as Sanctifier, titles which are appropriately directed to Father, Son and Holy Spirit, respectively. Thus the dogmatic synthesis of the *Catechism* has a triadic structure. First comes a 'paterological' section on the almighty Father, the Creator; next a 'christological' section on the Son, our Lord and Saviour, and finally a 'pneumatological' section on the Holy Spirit, in the 'holy Church', which is his chosen instrument. In Part Two, the

---

[5] Ibid., 12.

Catechism describes how divine salvation, as realised once for all in Jesus Christ and by his Spirit, is rendered present in the sacred actions of the Church's Liturgy, and notably in her sacraments: here, then, the seven sacraments are to be contextualised in a prior account of the entire liturgical prayer of the Church, the exchange she makes with the Father through her high priest, the Mediator Jesus Christ. Thirdly, the moral section of the *Catechism*, on the life which goes with faith, will (very much in the spirit of St Thomas Aquinas) present beatitude, 'blessed happiness', as man's final, intrinsic goal (what else could be, since he is made in God's image?), and the ways to arrive there. Those 'ways' fall under the heading of action that is both right and free, assisted by both the law and the grace of God, and ordered to the expression of the twofold love-command of the New Testament (love of God, love of our neighbour), as deployed in all the realms of life signalled by the Ten Words of the Old. Finally, the fourth section offers a general account of prayer and its rôle in the Christian life prior to presenting its commentary on the *Pater noster* as a summary of the good things we are to hope for, the good things the Father has promised to give.

It might be said that the *Catechism* thus begins from faith (in revelation), moves on to love (in the sacraments, which are God's love-tokens, and the Commandments, which are our love-response) prior to finishing with hope. And this is not unfitting for an era when the Kingdom, though come in the risen Lord and his Spirit-indwelt Church, is come only under veils, not in glory. Still, we must not press such schematic analysis too far, since, as the Prologue itself remarks, the *Catechism* is meant to be read as a unity where any one affirmation may throw light on all the rest. Cross-references, and the very full indices of subjects at the end, assist this process. Two departures from standard typography also help in the wise use of the *Catechism*: factually informative but less essential matter is placed in smaller type; absolutely essential summaries are italicised. This is a book to be not only read but also *used*.

In its close the Prologue turns to the topic of the 'adaptation' of the *Catechism*, from Samoa to Samarkand, on which the pope

Alerting the Reader: The Authors' Prologue

also touched. The content of the *Catechism* will come out very differently in different cultures, for different age groups; it will be affected by differences in the accustomed spirituality and social and ecclesial situation of those to whom it is addressed. All such 'indispensable adaptations' are left to the future little catechisms that local churches may produce, and, especially, to the genius of the individual catechist.[6] However, lest we think that here is a recipe for the re-introduction of uncontrolled pluralism by the back door, the Prologue prefaces these remarks by emphasising the importance of doctrinal exposition. No catechesis, however 'adapted', is acceptable which substitutes for authentic doctrine such *ersatz* forms of religious education as the recounting or exchange of 'life-enhancing' experiences, or the telling of narratives which engage with the personal life-stories of teachers or pupils – and under this implied stricture may be considered even biblical narrative where this is conceived as separate from, or even counter-posed to, doctrine. Such experiential and narrative modes of pedagogy are fine as illustrative, exemplary; but they do not yield the essential content which catechetics considers. And in a ringing declaration, the authors of the Prologue assert (*vis-à-vis* those who would write off the *Catechism* therefore as abstract irrelevancy) that *precisely because* its stress lies on doctrinal exposition it will prove a very present help for the 'maturing of faith', its 'putting down roots in personal life' and its 'shining forth in personal conduct'.[7] And, in a final telling citation from the *Catechism* of St Pius V, the Prologue implicitly corrects those who think that when orthodoxy comes in through the door charity flies out through the window. The Preface to the old *Roman Catechism* – a text which could hardly be described as theologically impressionistic – locates the true goal of all doctrine and teaching in 'the love that never ends'.[8]

---

[6]Ibid., 24.
[7]Ibid., 23.
[8]*Roman Catechism*, Preface, 11.

III

*Professing the Faith: The Creed and Revelation**

As already mentioned, the first book of the *Catechism*, on the Creed, opens with an account of what divine revelation, and its subjective correlate, faith, may be. If it is to avoid what is sometimes called a 'positivistic' view of revelation, whereby God's self-communication suddenly erupts into human ken all unprepared, like the volcanic island of Surtsey which surfaced to observers' astonishment off the coast of Iceland, the *Catechism* must provide some account of how the human animal is 'open' to God, and capable of receiving a word from his Creator should it be offered him. And this it does by making its own the venerable language of the human heart's 'natural desire' for God. It is the metaphysical nature of the human creature, as evinced in the restlessness of the heart recorded by St Augustine, that it can find no fully satisfying truth, nor enduring happiness, except in communion with God. The imaginative intuition of this massive fact about the human condition underlies the often impressive – though sometimes bizarre and even repulsive – religious beliefs and behaviour which the discipline variously known as comparative religion, the history of religions and religious phenomenology studies. Both when sublime and when (in the common or garden sense of the word) pathetic, the data of religion-at-large testify to the fact that man, at his best and his worst, is essentially a religious being. That was at any rate part of the point St Paul made to the Athenian

* = *Catechism*, Paragraphs 26–197.

intelligentsia when he addressed them on the Acropolis (Acts 17:26–28). Catholic Christians do not approve of all religion *in et per se*; like every other human product it is a curate's egg, good in parts. Irreligion, or hostility to religion, has a variety of causes, not all of which, then, show up the anti-religious objectors in an unfavourable light. The *Catechism* lists them as: religious ignorance and indifference; over-absorption in the world and its riches; Godless philosophies and ideologies ; a guilty refusal to face the light of God (all factors of a disreputable kind, evidently), but also: a sentiment of revolt aroused by the world's evil, and the bad example sometimes given by believers (considerations which even up the balance sheet to some extent). The general conclusion is that religion, taken as a sheer fact of human life, is fine so long as it is animated by a genuine search for God, and characterised by a strenuous intellectual effort, by uprightness of will, and the capacity to learn from other people.

A number of 'ways' for mind and heart, working in conjunction, to uncover the existence of God in, with, and through the existence of the world and the reflector mirror of human experience have proved their merits, and the *Catechism* summarises these (rather too briefly to be helpful to teachers without some training in the philosophy of religion, or at least classical apologetics). It suggests two main ways. One is 'cosmological' – for pagans themselves, as St Paul pointed out in the Letter to the Romans (1:19–20), have perceived the world as a defective imitation of the divine perfections, and here the *Catechism* cites St Augustine's sermons in singling out the *beauty* of the natural world as an appeal from its glorious Creator. The other is 'anthropological' – for man experiences his own soul, whose spirituality is attested by his concern with truth, beauty, morality and the open-ended nature of his strivings, as something inexplicable in a reductionistically conceived, purely material, universe, and so must posit its source in God alone. In each case, it is a question of seeing being (the world's or our own) as *derived* or *participated* – as essentially a *relation* to the One who alone is intrinsic being, namely, God. The *Catechism* recommends approaching these (and doubtless other) philosophical, yet also experiential, 'ways' to God in a generous spirit of letting them accumulate probative force, of treating them as convergent.[1] Two caveats must be entered. First, it is one thing to be able to know the existence of God; quite another to enter intimately into his life (the goal which revelation addresses). Secondly, while the Catholic Church teaches as solemn dogma the natural knowability of God – which is founded on man's divine imagehood, she also recognises that, in the concrete conditions of culture here or there, this, like many other religious and moral truths open in principle to human appropriation, may be a discovery beyond the resources of many. That is why – as the *Catechism* will later show – divine revelation has wisely included within its content not only truths beyond the wit of man to fathom, for they deal with God's gracious design for the world and its conditions in his own blessed life, but also truths that lie already within the compass of human intelligence – truths that are in principle knowable and yet, owing to the darkening of intellect and the corruption of will that follow on the Fall, and the errors and misprisions these bring in their wake in the history of culture, would go by default without some more-than-natural bringing to mind.

Before turning to that revelation, one last question awaits, and that is, How may we *speak* of that God whose existence reason can infer, and experience apprehend? Here the *Catechism* makes its own the position of St Thomas, founded as that is on the Sapiential tradition of the Bible. If 'from the greatness and beauty of creatures their Author is known by analogy' (Wisdom 13:5), then it should be possible, on the basis of the multifarious if limited perfections found in creatures, to forge a language of pure or unlimited perfection for the divine reality which is their Source. More might have been offered, from within the resources of Christian Scholasticism, to help the reader grasp the grammar of discourse about God. Nonetheless, what is essential is said. The divine 'names' – the True, the Good, the Beautiful – prompted by the capacity of these 'transcendental', category-bridging words to advert to

[1]This is, as it happens, the approach taken to this subject in my *Grammar of Consent. The Existence of God in Christian Tradition* (Notre Dame, Indiana, and Edinburgh 1991), where fuller materials on this topic are provided.

the most significant dimensions of reality as such, do attain God as the fullness of being, 'absolute value', yet such is the infinite qualitative difference between the Uncreated and the created that we never master the *mode* or *way* these terms apply to him. Coming at him from many angles as our discourse does we miss, in particular, the total simplicity of God – the fact that everything he *has* by way of attribute he *is*. And making its own two highpoints of mediaeval theology, one a conciliar statement, the other a piece of personal thought, the *Catechism* declares with the Fourth Lateran Council that where there is any similarity between God and creatures the dissimilarity is greater, and with St Thomas that what we know of him is only what he is not and how creatures relate to him. In his positive mystery, in other words, God's very light *encloses* him in its robe of glory.

The *Catechism* has not yet reached, however, that additional, complementary kind of knowledge of God which is its real subject: God's free design, eternally established in his lovingkindness, to reveal his Fatherly mystery by sending to the world his beloved Word or Son, and their Holy Spirit.

Unlike human beings, God can communicate not only through words but also via entire events. But if it be true that actions speak louder than words, words are still required for actions to be interpreted. We can expect, then, that the God of all being, who can move his creatures both externally, through his providential will, and internally, through his inspiration of their faculties, will make use of a combination of events and language in order to declare his hand. Events interpreted by language; language finding its referent in events: these will be the means of his encounter with us. In the clarification one brings to another, the divine design of revelation begins to stand out. Little by little, more areas of the tapestry are filled in, till we can glimpse the harmonious whole. Or, in a more personalist metaphor, drawn from the third century Church Father Irenaeus of Lyons, the educational method or 'pedagogy' of the Word of God, establishes, in the successive phases of the history of salvation, an increasing familiarity between humanity and God. The Word of God gradually familiarises man with the true God who himself becomes 'accustomed' to taking up his dwelling with man.

The *Catechism* speaks of four stages in the creation of this reciprocal relationship, this 'covenant' – to use the language of Scripture which it makes its own. A rich account of the *Noachic* covenant sounds unusual today – but would not have done so to the Fathers. When the original cosmic covenant implicit in the act of creation is imperilled by the spread of human sin, the scale of whose well-merited judgment is symbolised in Scripture by the great Ancient Near Eastern flood, God makes a covenant through Noah with still pagan humanity. Initiating the 'time of the Gentiles', which will last, for non-Jews, till the first proclamation of the Gospel, the Noachic covenant takes as its instrument the plurality of 'nations' or basic human groups, which are actively integrated into the general scheme of God's Providence through angel guardians. The division of humanity acts as a break on hubris, for the total pooling of human energy by fallen man – as distinct from man re-made in charity – could only mean a robbers' pact. Yet throwing a spanner in the works of those who would build a Tower of Babel – a universal human project reaching for the heavens but without God – leaves other problems untouched. Entrusting humanity to the cultural genius of its 'nations' opens the door to polytheism, the worship of the forms of transcendence generated by the corporate imagination of each people, and also collective self-worship, the idolatry of national apotheosis. The Noachic covenant can only be, therefore, a provisional 'economy': it is not an enduring but a makeshift case of the arrangements God mercifully makes to help man towards salvation. And yet, as the *Catechism* records, it produced the striking 'pagan saints' of the Hebrew Bible, from Abel to Job. Such 'holy pagans' are unthinkable without the graces offered to the human race in Noah. The way the *Catechism* deals with this neglected topic, which is relevant both to the Catholic assessment of the salvific value of the non-Abrahamic faiths, and to a political theology of nationalism and its woes, is a good example of its exegetical method: it treats Scripture as an overarching unity, taking different chronological stages in the emergence of the biblical literature, and varying sub-traditions among its texts as essentially subordinate to a global view of its contents. Not to be taken necessarily as assaulting other concepts of exegesis, which use other tools for other ends, it continues the impetus of those elements in modern biblical scholarship which emphasise the importance of the Canon – the identification of this *set of texts,* in the time, more or less, of its making as essentially parts of an organic whole, and the significance of the *tradition of interpretation* (in this case, that of the Church Fathers) to which the texts gave rise.

Only with the *Abrahamic* covenant are the first abiding structures of the divine plan for the resumption of humankind into unity with God and with itself at last put in place. Abram is called forth from the sophisticated urban civilisation of the Tigris–Euphrates valley, into the life of a nomadic figure, suited to serve as depositary of the promise for a new humanity yet to be born. As Abraham, with a new name, he will be the 'father of a multitude of peoples' (Genesis 17:5), and onto this stock of the ancestor of the Jewish people will be grafted one day the pagan nations, now become believers. Here, as in the attendant reminder of how the patriarchs and prophets of the Old Testament, beginning with Abraham himself, have traditionally been venerated in the Church as saints of the old covenant (though with the exception of some Religious Orders and the Latin patriarchate of Jerusalem, this is more honoured in the breach than in the observance in the modern Roman liturgy), we are given the first taste of the *Catechism's* high doctrine of Jewry: the warm, familial accents with which it speaks of the ancient people of God.

The *Mosaic* covenant, seen as the divine means of forming that people of Israel, whose eponymous ancestor was Abraham's son's son, enables the *Catechism* to rehearse the most doctrinally vital themes of the Old Testament. The covenant with Moses has as its precondition the divine freeing of Israel from slavery in Egypt, and as its consequences the gift of the Law, whereby the Jewish people could recognise and serve the provident and just God, and that future orientation (its basis not spelled out in the *Catechism* but consisting perhaps in the implications of the divine Name, disclosed on Sinai as 'I am, who will be with you', Exodus 3:14) which issued eventually in the messianic hope for a Saviour. Israel is a priestly people, carrying the Name of God through an ignorant antiquity, and remains the 'elder brother' both of Christians and Muslims. Most importantly, through his servants the prophets God aroused in his people the hope for a 'new and eternal Covenant' (words taken from the prayer of consecration of the Eucharistic elements in the Roman rite), a Covenant as wide as all the nations and as deep as the most tangled roots of the heart. The most steadfast bearers of this hope were those called in Hebrew the *anawim*: the 'poor of the Lord', the lowly of heart who expected little benefit from this-worldly causes. The *Catechism*, taking a cue from St Luke's Gospel, finds them summed up in the Blessed Virgin Mary.

The *Messianic* covenant, made in Jesus Christ, is this long-awaited definitive fulfilment of the plan of God for a needy world. If the Jewish hope had taken two basic forms, one for the appearing of a human agent who could represent the fullness of God's purpose for history, and the other a visitation of God himself, to strike at the world's evils and enhance its joys by the coming of his 'Day', then both – the one from 'below' and the one from 'above' – are fulfilled simultaneously in the coming of the incarnate divine Word, at once the eternal, perfect expression of the Father and the Jewish Messiah. Necessarily, with him, as God's own self-utterance, revelation is brought to its climax and its end, for no further increment can swell totality. All that can still be expected is, firstly, the *glorious* disclosure of what is now given fully but in lowliness (which will happen at the parousia, the Second Coming); secondly, the fuller explicitation, by the process known as doctrinal development, of what was tacit in the revelation in Christ; and thirdly, those divine leadings, sometimes called 'private revelations' whereby *the* revelation, completed in him, may in various of its aspects be more vividly grasped and lived in different ages of the Church.

The apostolic preaching is the means whereby the plenary revelation in Jesus Christ came to be transmitted throughout those ages. The *Catechism* defines it in the terms laid down by the Dogmatic Constitution of the Second Vatican Council on Divine Revelation, *Dei Verbum*: it is a passing on of the Gospel by both non-written means – oral preaching, example, and dominically founded institutions – and written means, the 'apostolic writings' of the New Testament. Rather more clearly than *Dei Verbum*, the *Catechism* defines the apostolic *tradition*, seen from the Gospel beginnings to our own time, as the sum total of the apostolic *preaching* and the subsequent process, initiated by that preaching, which is guarded and defined by the apostolic *succession*. The continuing traditioning of the Gospel, entrusted to the bishops as the apostles' successors, is a theandric reality, at once divine and human, as the Father's self-communication, in Son and Spirit, brings the Word of Christ to life in believers' hearts through the doctrine, life and cultus of the Church, closely linked though not identical, as these are with the sacred Scriptures. Like *Dei Verbum*, the *Catechism* considers Scripture and Tradition to be two differentiated aspects of a single reality. Very much in the manner of the French Dominican Yves Congar, its authors find the particular, contingent expressions of Tradition (in the singular, with a t majuscule) which are the traditions (in the plural, with a t minuscule) – theological, disciplinary, liturgical, devotional – to be so many media in which the one light of Tradition is refracted.[2] Though themselves deficient and even, taken individually, dispensable, they are the culturally specific forms in which the trans-cultural meanings of Tradition are embodied. Just so, were one to seek after, for instance, the body of knowledge now found in natural science, counsel might be given against one textbook or some practitioner. But to direct a 'hermeneutic of suspicion' against all textbooks and all practitioners would be effectively to disable oneself from ever understanding science at all.

The delicate question of how to identify Tradition in the traditions brings the *Catechism* to the topic of the magisterium – which is the Catholic way of answering the query thus posed. Although the deposit of faith – revelation in Jesus Christ – has been entrusted to the whole Church, its authoritative interpretation is the work of the doctrinal magisterium, the pope and bishops considered in their teaching office. (It is sometimes said that calling a group of people by the name of

---

[2] Y. M.-J. Congar, O.P., *Tradition and Traditions* (E.t. London 1966); cf. my *Yves Congar* (London and Wilton, CT 1989), pp. 26–51.

an activity is a grammatical solecism which points up the theological peculiarity of the 'official' Catholic view of how doctrine is defined and defended. But the usage differs not at all from referring to a British prime minister and his cabinet as 'The Government'.) The *Catechism's* account of that magisterium, its rôle of servant *vis-à-vis* the Word of God, and of 'teacher and mistress' *vis-à-vis* the people of God, is taken straight out of *Dei Verbum*, for the most part in the form of bare citation. Only in one point does the *Catechism* go beyond the Council, and that is in an appeal to the inspired theology of the Fourth Gospel. Conscious, no doubt, of the need in the current anti-dogmatic mood of much of the Church public, under the influence of liberal spirits among Catholic journalists, teachers and clergy, to defend the high profile given to authoritative doctrine in this *Catechism* of catechisms, the authors insist on the 'organic link' between dogma and spiritual life. The dogmas light up our journey of faith, making our footsteps sure, while inversely, if our spiritual life is *comme il faut* mind and heart will spontaneously fall open to receive the radiance of dogma. Here the *Catechism* transposes into terms of the 'splendour of doctrine' what the Johannine Christ has to say about the 'truth [that] will make you free' (John 8:32). Otherwise, the teaching given here on such matters as the supernatural sense of faith, growth in the understanding of faith, and the inter-connected character of Tradition, Scripture and magisterium is taken, without comment, from that most recent of the ecumenical Councils of the Church.

One might have thought that the *Catechism* would now have done with the topic of the formal nature, as distinct from the material content, of revelation. But, as if to emphasise that, despite its high doctrine of dogma and magisterium, the Catholicism it will present is through and through a *biblical* religion, it finishes with a lengthy section on the interpretation of Scripture. We will not be far wrong in tracing this decision to a concern with some recent products of Catholic biblical scholarship, and the effect these may have, once popularised, on catechetics. After all, not long after the appearance of the *Catechism*, the Pontifical Biblical Commission produced a lengthy document of its own on the Catholic approach to exegesis, with an introduction by the chairman of the Commission for the Catechism, Cardinal Ratzinger. *The Interpretation of the Bible in the Church*, though directed to professional exegetes and written, accordingly, in a more technical terminology, turns out to have the same basic message as these sections of the *Catechism*. For its burden is that, valuable as are the 'principal procedures' of the historical-critical method and at least occasionally illuminating as are those 'synchronic' rather than 'diachronic' kinds of Bible study which study the texts as rhetoric, narrative and a system of signs (semiotics), fidelity to the very Judaeo-Christian tradition of which the Bible is itself the witness will lead the Catholic exegete to take as the principal aim of his study the 'deepening of faith'. Catholic exegesis, this document maintains, 'does not have the right to become lost, like a stream of water, in the sands of a hypercritical analysis'. Instead, it must contribute to an 'ever more authentic transmission of the content of the inspired Scriptures'.[3] The *Catechism's* own approach, fully cognate with this conclusion, stresses the inspired nature of the Scriptures (which are not, then, on all fours with every other text that happens to have come down to us from the ancient world); the hermeneutical importance of the notion that the Holy Spirit is the primary interpreter of Scripture; the significance of the biblical Canon, as an articulation of Scripture's unity in diversity; and the need for an 'actualisation' of the message of the biblical authors which will be spiritually life-giving for today's Church. Basically, only the Church as the Bride of Christ is the adequate reader of Scripture considered as the Word of God written, whose riches belong at the feet of Christ, the Word of God incarnate, the true centre of the biblical revelation.[4]

And so we come to the human response to revelation: faith. Faith, the *Catechism* declares, is the (only) 'adequate' response to revelation. Contrary to its popular reputation as a vague

[3]Pontifical Biblical Commission, *The Interpretation of the Bible in the Church* (Rome 1994), Conclusion.

[4]Compare my 'François Dreyfus on Scripture read in Tradition' in *Scribe of the Kingdom. Essays on Theology and Culture* (London 1994), I. pp. 32–77 for further comment.

sentiment with distinctly questionable cognitive credentials, faith is an exactly precise attunement of man's subjective faculties – mind and heart – to the divine invitation which revelation comprises. This is not to say, however, that one crucial aspect of the secularist's poor opinion of faith is misplaced, for the text goes on to underline the character of faith as not only obedience (to God) but even *submission*. In an anthropocentric world, where man is the measure of all things, this is fighting talk. True, in modern philosophy and literary culture tendencies may be detected which displace or 'de-centre' humankind from the pivotal position in the construing of the world and its meaning which man has occupied since the Renaissance. Most of these, however, mount their attack on modern humanism from angles which would make them unsatisfactory allies to orthodox Catholicism: stressing, for instance, the priority of 'structures' over 'persons', or, again, calling into question the unique status of the human species as the crown of the animal creation. And indeed the most thoroughgoing of these assaults on an older version of human civilisation has targeted in particular the notion of the *logos*, or pre-existing meaning, which, in its religious form, was raised in the apostolic age, through the instrumentality of St John's Gospel, to the dignity of a title for the eternal Son of God. The *Catechism*, in effect, justifies its emphasis on obedience to the Word of divine revelation by the consideration that its 'truth is guaranteed by God, who is Truth itself'. The 'sweet primal Truth', as the fourteenth century Italian doctor of the Church Catherine of Siena called her Lord and Maker, holds out so abundant a feast of veridical meaning and right judgment that human intelligence loses nothing of its dignity – rather the contrary – in making a 'free submission' thereto.

The ecumenical Creed – the Symbol of faith produced by the Councils of Nicaea I and Constantinople I in 325 and 381 respectively – is couched in the plural ('we believe') in Greek, in the singular ('I believe') in Latin. The *Catechism* exploits this accident of linguistic history to set forth in turn the personal and the communitarian dimensions of believing. Under the heading of 'I believe', it proved possible to treat, first, of such living archetypes of faith as Abraham (whom the Roman

Canon calls 'our father in faith') and the Blessed Virgin Mary (addressed by an old Dominican litany as 'faith of all the faithful'); secondly, the peculiar force of the prepositional phrase 'believing *in*' – for the act of faith is always directed to the three-personed God, worthy, and a thousand times worthy, of our love and trust, and thirdly a number of typical characteristics of faith. To outline these: faith is a symbiotic act in which the intrinsic evidence of divine revelation, the extrinsic signs of credibility which accompany it (miracle, prophecy, the amazing spread of the community of the Resurrection witnesses, and suchlike) and the interior activity of the Holy Spirit at the quick of our personalities (all divine factors), mesh with the movement of our intellect and will, in ready, uncoerced adherence to the Sun of truth and goodness now appearing on our horizon (the human elements). The *Catechism's* doctrine of the personal act of faith combines St Anselm's stress on faith's tendency to seek more and more to *understand* what it believes with an emphasis, more easily associated with the Franciscan tradition, on the complementary dynamism which leads faith to mounting ardour in the *love* of God. Indebted to the conciliar tradition of Vatican I and Vatican II for its insistence that the eyes of faith open onto the mysteries of the divine plan, seen not as isolated truths but as closely related to each other and to Christ, revelation's heart, the text also makes its own St Basil the Great's affirmation that faith is a foretaste of the joy and light of the beatific vision – something more customarily associated by Western Catholic theologians with St Thomas' notion of faith as *semen gloriae*, the 'seed of glory'. This is just one point among many where the *Catechism* turns for inspiration to the Eastern Christian tradition – one Oriental Catholic commentator has spoken in this connexion of the *Catechism's* (predominant) Western 'stamp', yet still strongly discernible Eastern 'imprint'.[5] Not that St Thomas is completely neglected in the account of personal faith: typically Thomist is the insistence that, though revealed truth may seem obscure to

---

[5] G.-P. Noujelm (Maronite patriarchal vicar of Sarba-Kesrouan, Lebanon), 'Reflections on the *Catechism of the Catholic Church* – 4', *l'Osservatore Romano* (English edition), 24 March 1993, p. 10.

human reasoning and experience, it is in fact more certain than any other truth, because known through a medium – the divine light – more epistemologically exalted than the usual medium of our understanding – the light of human reason.

When analysed, it turns out that the *Catechism's* section on the individual act of faith moves in a broadly chronological way, tracing the factors involved in the genesis and constitution of faith, *en route* to faith's term in the face-to-face vision of glory. The central segment is, quite properly therefore, taken up with the soteriological necessity of faith and of perseverance in faith. For guilty creatures to be rendered just and asked into the divine family by adoption, they must believe in Jesus Christ and the One who sent him – for only by grace and favour of God in Christ is such a dizzy reversal of spiritual fortune possible. And if at this point, though briefly, the *Catechism* takes up the concern of the sixteenth century Reformers with justification by faith, it also makes clear, over against much classical Protestant soteriology, that the gift can be lost. To persevere to the end cannot be presumed certain: it calls for a strenuous effort of what the Byzantine tradition terms *synergia*, man's co-operation with saving grace. The *Catechism* sets out what this involves very fully: it is a matter of feeding ourselves on the Word of God, praying for an increase of faith; setting faith to work in charity; finding support in the theological virtue of hope; and, last but not least, being sustained by the wider faith of the Church.

To that ecclesial faith – the corporate 'We believe' – the *Catechism* now turns. The actual content of what it is we believe in faith is not excogitated from our own resources but comes to us from the corporate mind of the only adequate subject of faith, the Church. Whereas salvation comes from God alone, we are born into the life of faith, through Baptism, from the Church whom we refer to accordingly as *Mother* Church. The *Catechism* is especially anxious to restore to currency the vocabulary of *Ecclesia mater*, which came so readily to the lips of patristic Christians and indeed of modern Catholics in an earlier generation. The motherhood of the Church, when not simply registered formally but felt on the pulse, in the blood, preserves us from a dessicatedly institutional view of ecclesial communion. There are indeed inalienable institutional elements in the life of the Church; but they are abiding gifts of the Lord to his Spouse, to enable her more effective mothering of her children. At the same time, the perception of the Church as mother puts to flight the delusion that she is a 'patriarchal' institution, the fact notwithstanding that her ordained servants play the symbolic rôle of the (male) Christ in her (female) regard: indeed, seen rightly, the restriction of the priesthood to those of male gender confirms the Church's essentially female character.

And if mother, then educator. The Church teaches in two primary ways: by initiating her sons and daughters into the memory of Christ's words, which she ponders in her heart, and by confessing the faith of the apostles which she proclaims in her preaching. She is a unique linguistic community, teaching the language of faith so as to introduce us to the understanding of faith, and, more than understanding, faith's life. Making ample use of St Irenaeus' comments on the apostolic tradition, the *Catechism* affirms the over-arching unity of this community, despite its many tongues: it is vital to the *Catechism's* whole project, and to meeting the urgent needs of world Catholicism at this juncture in time, that we stress the unicity of the language of the Church, while noting that speakers of one language may have many dialects, and, *a fortiori*, accents.

Although the Creed of the *oikoumenê*, the Great Church spread throughout the world, is, above all, the Creed of Nicaea–Constantinople, the decision was taken to deploy the doctrinal matter in the Catechism's first book through the agency of the Old Roman or Apostles' Creed. Hinted at in the text of the *Catechism* itself the reasons were explained more fully elsewhere by Cardinal Ratzinger. Feeling that the Nicene–Constantinopolitan Creed, recited at Mass on Sundays and greater feast days, is essentially 'a bishops' creed which then afterwards also became the creed of the community gathered to celebrate the Eucharist', the authors of the *Catechism* preferred in the end the *Apostolicum*, despite its more local origin as the creed of the church of the city of Rome. For this is an exclusively *baptismal* creed, and thus one linked more closely to catechesis, which is itself either 'an introduction to

Baptism or a renewal of the life of the baptised'.⁶ And since the regional baptismal creeds of the Church have marked family resemblances, the local affiliations of the Old Roman Creed would, it was hoped, prove inoffensive. And if we enquire, What *is* a 'Creed' anyway? the book has two answers. In the ancient world, a *symbolon* was an object one half of which could be presented by, say, a messenger to the holder of the other half as a sign of authentication, or recognition. A Creed, *symbolon* in Greek, is thus a 'sign of recognition and communion among believers'. Alternatively or complementarily, less etymologically and more simply, it is a 'collection of the principal truths of the faith'.

And just as the personal act of faith has been shown to have as its *object* the Holy Trinity – for faith is always *in* the Father, the one God, by his Son, in their Holy Spirit, and so in those three Persons inseparably, so now the *content* of the faith, articulated in the clauses of the Creed, is declared to be Trinitarian likewise. And no historian of the Creeds is likely to disagree. Everything the Creed says can be, and is, brought under the heading of belief in the Father and his work, the Son and his mission, the Holy Spirit and his saving activity.

---

⁶J. Ratzinger, 'The *Catechism of the Catholic Church* and the optimism of the redeemed', *Communio* XX. 3 (1993), p. 481.

IV

*Professing the Faith: The Creed on the Father**

The Creed begins with the Father as source of the life of the Trinity, and his creative work as the foundation of all the other divine actions for our salvation. The confession of the one and only God, the God who is uniquely one, is the most basic *credendum* of Israel and so of the Church. The *Catechism* does not fail to record then the *Shema*, the faithful Jew's daily prayer: 'Hear, O Israel: the Lord our God is one Lord; and you shall love the Lord your God, with all your heart, and with all your soul, and with all your might' (Deuteronomy 6:4–5). The progressive revelation of the divine Name discloses the further attributes of God's sole Essence in such a way as to enfold in a nascent communion of life the Revealer and those to whom he is revealed. Here the rich ores of Old Testament biblical theology are mined so as to display at one and the same time the Hebrew Bible's doctrine of God and its understanding of his purposes and characteristic 'style'. The God of the Fathers must be a God who 'remembers' the patriarchs and his promises to them, One who is compassionately faithful. Similarly, the God who gives his Name at the Burning Bush as 'I am He who is' must be raised up beyond all human description, yet ready and willing to be present to his people for their salvation. Precisely at the moment of that mysterious theophany in the desert, the Mosaic tradition registers the utter holiness of the God before whom the prophet removes his sandals in humility

* = *Catechism*, Paragraphs 198–421.

and penitence (Exodus 3:5–6) – and here the *Catechism* looks ahead to the confirmation of this divine attribute in the Temple vision of Isaiah (Isaiah 6:5) and the withdrawal of Peter, overwhelmed, at the divine signs worked by Jesus (Luke 5:8). When the revelatory event of the Mosaic experience is resumed after the rupture of Israel's temporary lapse into idolatry at the foot of Sinai, the divine Name is further glossed as He who is 'merciful and gracious, slow to anger and abounding in steadfast love and faithfulness' (Exodus 34:6) – which again suggests a glance into the future when the God who is thus 'rich in mercy' (Ephesians 2:4) will send his Son, with whom he shares the divine Name, to raise up a fallen world.

The *Catechism* synthesises the divine attributes, as ascribed by Israel to the one God, in two terms: truth and love. The Old Testament witness to God's truth as absolute wisdom and total fidelity to his own word, on the one hand, and, on the other, unconditional love, the eternal archetype of the best relations of children with parents, lovers with their spouses, confirms, and more than confirms, the postulates of rational divinity that God is the fullness of being and of all perfections. In due course, in the New Testament, the Son and Spirit will come to render testimony to the divine truth and to reveal the inner life of the Godhead as an exchange of love. Meanwhile, the *Catechism* draws the practical consequence of its teaching on the one God: for such foundational beliefs bring consequences for living in their train. To believe in this primal Reality is, among other things, to live by putting him first.

But the one God is for the Creed the *Father*, and since his Fatherhood, in the Holy Spirit, is essentially the generation of his eternal Son and Word, the disclosure of the Fatherly qualities of the true God finds its fulfilment in the self-revelation of the Holy Trinity, which is thus the *Catechism's* next topic. Trinitarianism is the specifically Christian doctrine of God; citing emblematically the sixth century Burgundian Church Father Caesarius of Arles, *Fides omnium christianorum in Trinitate consistit*: 'the faith of all Christians rests on the Trinity', a quotation from his own *Exposition of the Creed*. The revelation of the single divine Name in its threefoldness enfolds within itself the entire story of salvation.

The *Catechism* is quite correct to regard the naming of God in Fatherly terms as quite transformed in meaning by the revelation of the Son's co-eternal being. For this implies that God is essentially Father – that is, generativity, spontaneous self-donation – *even before the world was made*. This introduces into the Christian doctrine of God a warmth not found in Judaism or Islam; at the same time, while in no way undermining the gratuitousness of God's creation of the world (his sharing of his being with finite creatures is a free gift) it removes all arbitrariness from the act of creation. Creating is the very thing we might expect the Father of the Word to do.

But this is not to say that the ascription of the name 'Father' tells us nothing directly about the God-world relationship. Even before we know of the Son's eternal origin the divine 'Fatherhood' is eloquent of God's transcendent origination of the world, and his authoritative solicitude for it in Providence. The image of God as 'Mother' is also scriptural and bespeaks, as the *Catechism* points out (Paragraph 239), the intimacy of God's relation to creatures, and so his immanence within the world (as distinct from transcendence over it). Though the *Catechism* does not say so, this contrast explains the primacy of male-gender imagery for God. God's transcendence of the world not only conditions his deity (his being precisely *God*); it also makes possible his immanence within it. Thus for biblical revelation the discontinuity between God and the world, signified by language in the male gender (the gender farther from the process of 'birthing') is a more primordial truth than that of his ('her') continuity with the world, signified by female-gender language. In himself, of course, as the *Catechism* points out, God is neither male or female: that fact does not, however, justify *our* transgression of the (theologically crucial) rules of biblical discourse.[1]

Coming to the substance of the doctrine: the Father's self-revelation in the Son as the *Abba*, 'dear Father' of One who is his perfect Image, dogmatised in the two ecumenical Councils of the fourth century, is perpetuated in the revelation of both

---

[1] See R. W. Jenson, *Triune Identity. God according to the Gospel* (Philadelphia 1982), pp. 15–16.

Father and Son by the Holy Spirit, whose own divinity was confessed by the second of those Councils in the wake of the first. Emphasising the 'economic' or functional rôles of the Son and the Spirit in the further disclosure of the Godhead, the *Catechism* rehearses the very approach which the Fathers of that golden age of patristic theology themselves took. For how can One who reveals God not be themself God? At the same time, and as the formulation of this question implies, the economic manifestation of the second and third Persons in no way reduces their being to that of modes of the Father's life: a point to be made explicitly when the *Catechism* considers their reciprocal relations. The Church's preferred terminology here, though philosophical in origin (the key terms are 'substance', 'person' and 'relation'), involves no subordination of the faith to some merely human wisdom for the conciliar tradition has given a 'new and unprecedented meaning to these terms, which from then on would be used to signify an ineffable mystery'.[2] The language of *substance* is invoked to confess that the divine Being is one: the Persons do not divide the single divinity for each is wholly God. The Trinity, in other words, is 'consubstantial'. The language of *person* is invoked to confess the real distinction between Father, Son and Spirit, signified by their differentiated origins: the Father without a Source, the Son generated by the Father, the Holy Spirit proceeding from the Father and the Son – or, as the Eastern tradition would have it, from the Father-of-the-Son; that is, *through* the Son. Though by implication the *Catechism* stigmatises as erroneous those elements in the Byzantine and modern Eastern Orthodox tradition which would insist on a strict Monopatrism, excluding all rôle for the Son in the Spirit's coming to be, it regards the Latin *Filioque* and the Oriental *per Filium* as complementary theologies. While the order in which the Persons are named – Father, Son, Spirit – already implies an indebtedness of the Spirit to the Son, the Western theology gives higher profile to the consubstantial communion of the Persons. This is an advantage, but it does not amount to exclusive legitimacy. Finally, the language of *relation* is invoked to confess the

[2]Paragraph 251.

mutual reference of the Persons to each other in that blessed communion of knowledge and love. The *Catechism* could have chosen no better text from all the Christian centuries to illustrate this mystery than the passage from the *Orations* of St Gregory Nazianzen where that fourth century Greek Father tells the catechumens that he has barely begun to think of God's unity when – lo! – he is plunged into the splendour of the Trinity, and has hardly started to think of the Trinity when – behold! – the Unity grasps and fills him.

We have already seen from the *Catechism's* Prologue that absolutely foundational to its conception is the truth of faith that this same 'Light, blessed Trinity, primordial Unity', as the Office hymn of Vespers calls God, freely planned to communicate to rational creatures the glory of his own blissful life. Given the divine unity, all three Persons will be at work in the whole of God's activity of creation and redemption. But given the irreducible threeness of the Persons, each will so act according to his personal 'property': the Father paternally, the Son filially, the Spirit pneumatically. The missions of the Son and of the Holy Spirit in, respectively, the Incarnation of the first and the Giving of the second, are the principal manifestation in the world of the inner-divine properties of these Persons. The divine Economy is at once, therefore, common and personal; it makes known both the unitary nature of the Persons and their distinctiveness. The life to which it invites human beings is one of communion with each Person, but inseparably from the others. In a splendid *précis* of Johannine and Pauline triadology, the *Catechism* declares that 'Everyone who glorifies the Father does so through the Son in the Holy Spirit; everyone who follows Christ does so because the Father draws him and the Spirit moves him' (compare John 6:44; Romans 8:14).[3]

The Creed, however, calls the Father (and the *Catechism's* account of the Holy Trinity is but an investigation of the final implications, for New Testament faith, of the name 'Father') the 'Father *almighty*', and pause must be allowed to consider the issues raised by this adjective – notably, the problem of evil.

[3]Paragraph 259.

The last topic, theodicy, has aroused a vast literature; the *Catechism's* comments are notable for their austerity and restraint. In general, the terms in which the problem of evil has been posed, since the early Christian apologist Lactantius, entail the counterposing of the Father's goodness – virtually a tautology, for goodness is necessarily an attribute of One hailed as a perfect 'Father' – and his almightiness. Given evil, either an all-good God is not all-powerful, or an all-powerful God is not all-good.[4] The *Catechism* softens the force of this contrast from the outset by describing divine omnipotence as not only 'universal' and 'loving' – terms which, left to themselves, would if anything sharpen Lactantius' dilemma – but also *'mysterious'*. God's almighty power must be called 'mysterious' because only faith can recognise it when, in the words of St Paul, it is 'deployed in weakness' (II Corinthians 12:9).[5] Faith in the almighty Father can be severely tested by experiences of evil – and notably of suffering. God may seem absent or unable to impede evil's advance. Through the voluntary humiliation of the divine Son, and the glorious Resurrection which is not only its sequel but its result, the Father has revealed that, in the mysterious ways of his omnipotence, he conquers evil most fully by the appearance of submission to its power. This is a pregnant hint which it will require the fuller soteriological reflection of the central christological portion of the commentary on the Creed to tease out. Other ways of illuminating the issue of evil, burdensome to many God-seeking minds as it is, will be explored in the sections of the *Catechism*, shortly to follow, on 'creaturely defect' and original sin (see p. 41 below).

The next paragraphs, on the creative act, are as vital for the cosmology and anthropology of the *Catechism* as its comments on 'one God, the Father almighty' are for its theology strictly so called. A presentation of the 'hexaemeron', the six-day work

[4] Lactantius, *De ira Dei*, 13.
[5] The translation will be unfamiliar to Anglo-Saxon readers. Among the various possible senses of the Pauline verb, *telô*, the original French edition of the *Catechism* relies on that elected by the translators of the *Bible de Jérusalem*, masterwork of the Dominican Ecole Biblique in that city. The English edition by rendering from the Greek, replaces 'deployed' with 'made perfect' (Paragraph 268).

of the divine Craftsman, as described in Genesis, played a major part in the instruction of Christians in the patristic age, while the Genesis text forms the first reading at every vigil of the feasts of the Lord in the Byzantine Liturgy. As the *Catechism* remarks, the theology of the creation concerns the 'very foundations of human and Christian life'.[6] A serene welcome of contemporary investigation into the origins of the world, of life and of man on the part of astrophysicists, historical biologists and palaeontologists is coupled with an insistence that only the meta-scientific – *metaphysical* – assessment of the respective merits of the two chief competing explanatory theories – chance or God – can resolve the question descriptive science raises. Not that we should forget other stranger or darker speculations – about the becoming of the world as God's becoming, in pantheism, or its coming to be by way of a cosmic fall, in various forms of gnosticism, that have returned to the agenda in a 'New Age' setting as pluralistic as it is untutored.

It is a relief to turn from such alternatives and to renew, with the *Catechism*, one's sense of the Christian understanding of the act of creation. The topic unifies a cluster of themes: the origin and goal of creation in God, its order and goodness, as well as the special vocation of the human creature, betrayed by sin but not wholly mislaid for there remains the hope of salvation. These motifs are handled with increasing passion and fullness in the Old Testament literature, as the covenanted mercies of God with Israel and his first gift, existence itself, come to illumine one another. Here the *Catechism* recognises that, for the Scriptures, the divine origination of the world is not a mere metaphysical fact, however stupendous in scale, but the first revelation of the universal love of God for creatures.

By the Word of the Lord were the heavens made, and their host by the Breath of his mouth. The *Catechism* underlines the Trinitarian character of the world's making, essential if the creation is to be of itself a manifestation of the divine life. From the Letter to the Ephesians to the thirteenth century Franciscan doctor Bonaventure, and on again to the First Vatican Council, the tradition is unanimous that the world has been made for

[6]Paragraph 282.

the communication (not the augmentation) of God's glory. That superabundant Life and Wellspring of graciousness to which the mystery of creation directs us will be our felicity, though we can never increase his. The sheer gratuitousness of creation finds its full meaning, therefore, in the free gift of salvation by which God calls his creatures to enter his intimate life. That the creation is 'from nothing' tells us, moreover, that out of negativity God can draw positivity; from the death of the soul in sin and the death of the body in biological extinction the One who summoned into existence the things that were not can give life to the dead too (cf. Romans 4:17).

The world is not only living through God's Spirit, it is also ordered through his Word. The *Catechism* insists on the importance of certain theses in epistemology for the claim that man, God's image, can grasp the immanent wisdom in the world about him. It is because human intelligence shares in the light of the divine Mind that it can understand the words God speaks in the Word.

As this study has had occasion already to mention, the divine transcendence is the condition of possibility of the divine immanence, and the *Catechism* now spells this out on its own account. Only the infinite quality of God's excess of his creation can explain the utter interiority of his presence within it, *intimius intimo meo*, 'more intimate to me than I am to myself', as Augustine writes in the *Confessions*.[7] And that 'presence by immensity' – as the Thomist school calls it – can be taken soteriologically as the gauge and promise of God's continued shepherding of his creation: Providence, itself not simply a general and architectonic scheme rather along the lines of Hegel's *Phenomenology of Spirit* or Arnold Toynbee's *Study of History* but a knowing solicitude for every creature, something not only macrocosmic, then, but microcosmic also.

But the creation is not a pastoral idyll. The *Catechism* must counter-point its radiant music with elements of cacophony orchestrated in sombre tones. Return to the problem of evil sounds a note which will not fade until the final doxology in its closing paragraph.

---

[7] *Confessions* III. 6, xi.

The *Catechism* sees the problem of evil as in some way all-embracing: there is no point of Christian faith which does not relate to it. Its 'solution' is not so much a theoretical explanation as it is the highly practical response of God's redemptive intervention in the world through his Son and the Holy Spirit. And yet *some* theoretical mitigation of the force of the problem is possible – and must be, for otherwise it stands as an indictment of belief in an all-good and all-powerful God – a 'Father almighty'. So far as 'physical' evil is concerned – the pain and suffering found through natural causes in the world about us, it is not to impugn God's wise benevolence to say that he created not so much a perfect world as a world *en route* to its own ultimate perfection. And where 'moral' evil is in question – the pain and suffering inflicted by free agents, God permits what he otherwise abhors out of respect for the dignity of freedom he has given angels and men, and, in his almighty Providence, draws good out of such evil, whether here or hereafter. The super-abounding of grace which followed on the judicial murder of his Son-made-man, is the paradigm and the crown of this process. Since 'secondary causes' are real – because, that is to say, creatures are not only caused but *causers* – the relation between the world and God is a true drama, not a puppet-show. The world responds to God as he to the world, and the eventual result of this inter-action, its *dénouement*, is that all shall be well and all manner of things well, in the words of Mother Julian of Norwich, which is not to say, however, that an evil ever becomes itself a good.

And the world which God has thus sent on its way, not without struggle, to the eternal Sabbath of its final perfecting is a complex universe whose main dividing-line runs between 'heaven' and 'earth' – between the angelic creation, and the material world of which the human species is the (ontological if not moral) glory. Following the witness of Scripture, summarised at the Fourth Lateran Council (1215), the angels are better known by their office than in their nature, though tradition thinks of these mighty go-betweens in the commerce of God with man as intelligences coruscating with the power of will. Man came to consciousness in a universe where rational spirits preceded him, chiefly for good but also, alas, for evil.

The special virtue of the *Catechism's* angelology is its christocentric character. The angels are Christ's angels (cf. Matthew 25:31): the life of Christ, as presented by the Gospels is marked by an extreme concentration of angelic presences. A reflective theology would see in this the re-alignment of the angelic orders, conceived in their function as messengers, on the person of the God–man, who is the Mediator *par excellence* – the One in whom God and the visible world are rendered immediate to each other, and so the true centre of angelic activity. The *Catechism*, however, prefers not to speculate, even thus soberly, but to record the conviction of the Church that the angels of Christ continue to play a rôle in the dispensation which follows his atoning work – both through their 'guardianship' of his disciples and, most notably, at the Liturgy.

If a theological cosmology cannot do without the angels, that in no way detracts from the ecology of the visible creation but rather helps to contextualise it in a world which is not a diffused web of creaturely relations, simply, but a *uni-*verse, a totality with a single centre, God.

The visible cosmos is itself poised between the primordial moment, whose virtualities the Creator gradually unfolds, in their richness, variety and order, and a final goal, which consists in its taking up into the life of the Resurrection. The creation narratives of the Old Testament register symbolically the making of the first creation (treated as the six-day labouring of an artisan who takes his repose in contemplation of his achievement on the seventh). The *Catechism* does not claim for this prose-poem that it captures at any rate the rough outline of the successive origin of species. Instead, it praises the inspired authors for the more foundational truths about creation. To see creation steadily and see it whole, we need to keep in mind at one and the same moment truths which, if left each to themselves, would distort the perspective. Thus every creature has its own goodness and its proper perfection – and yet each lives in dependence on the rest: without *both* the intrinsic diversity of creatures *and* their reciprocal relations the beauty of the world (and *kosmos* shares a Greek root with *kosmêsis*, 'beautification') would not be. Again, all creatures – all *kinds* of creatures – are arranged on a ladder with humankind as its highest rung (the *Catechism* is not afraid of 'speciesism' in thus singling out man, with the Scriptures, as the image of God), but this metaphor of the vertical must not be taken as derogating from the 'horizontal' solidarity of all species, to which St Francis' *Canticle of the Creatures*, with its invocation of the earth, our 'mother', the sun our 'brother', water our 'sister', bears witness.

The Sabbath rest prescribed by the Hebrew Bible is described in exalted terms – and yet treated as *dépassé*. The creation is – in symbol speech – *for* the Sabbath: in other words, the worship of God is written into the very texture of the world, such that, where it becomes articulate in human praise the world itself attains its goal. The Sabbath must constitute, therefore, the 'heart' of the Torah, just as, for the Rule of Saint Benedict, nothing is to be preferred to the *opus Dei*, the work of God, the divine Liturgy. But the Sabbath, wonderful as it is, now finds itself transcended. The seventh day yields to the eighth, which is for the patristic theology of time both the day of Christ's Resurrection and the 'day' of the recreation of the whole world from the resources of his new life.

And this means, then, that the transfiguration of the original creation passes by way of the history and fate of a human being – and it is to *man* that the *Catechism* will turn for its final remarks on the creative activity of the Father. As already mentioned, the Book of Genesis sees in man the image of God. That metaphor, more pervasively present in the Scriptures than might at first appear, provides the ground work for the theological anthropology of the Church – her doctrine of the *humanum*.

Much ink has been spilt on the question of what it is that makes the human being God's image; the *Catechism* opts for the view, especially clearly expressed in the last books of St Augustine's treatise on the Trinity but widely represented in the patristic tradition at large, that man's divine imagehood lies in his capacity to know, love, and thus share the life of, God himself. And following St Catherine of Siena, the only explanation for *that* must be God's gratuitous goodness – in the strong language of her *Dialogues*, his *infatuation* with man. It is because human nature is in God's image that the individuated form of that nature is not merely a something but a someone – a person. And gathering up the fruits of reflection on selfhood, on the 'hypostatic' character of the human individual, from a variety of sources ancient and modern, the *Catechism* lists the distinctive qualities of persons: they are able to know and possess themselves, and thus can freely give themselves (for, again, one cannot give what one has not got), entering not only into communion with others like themselves but into covenant response, through faith and love, with the God in whose image they were made.

Most important for the coming chapters of the *Catechism* on Christology and ecclesiology – the work of the Son and the Spirit – but simply noted now *en passant*, this human nature is something deep and riddling (a 'mystery') on which we are fully enlightened only in the Word-made-human, Jesus Christ. Moreover, those who share it are on numerous counts *essentially one* – the human race is a unity in consideration of its origin, nature, earthly goal and mission, habitat, supernatural end and the means to achieve it, above all through union with the redeeming work of the same Jesus Christ. And that unity of the human race – at least in principle, indeed by reference to so many principles – is highly relevant to the divine project of the founding of the Church, which the Second Vatican Council will call the sacrament of the race's unity with itself in God.

More pressing at this point in the exposition of the Creed are those two great differentiations of human nature, body and soul, male and female. The anthropology of the *Catechism*, in tune with the conciliar tradition of mediaeval Catholicism, distinguishes the spiritual principle in the life of the human person – the soul – from the body, ascribing to the former direct divine creation and imperishability. This does not mean, however, that the human body is excluded from the dignity of imagehood of God, for the body is animated by the soul, and is its manifestation, its face. Other terms for facets of the internal differentiation of man such as 'spirit' and 'heart' are not the names of really distinct aspects of the human totality, but ways of alluding to, respectively, the soul's call to share supernatural life and the deep places of the person where the soul's liberty is mortgaged to this course or to that.

At the beginning of the race's history, male and female –

man and woman – were created not only together but for each other. Woman, in Genesis, is to be lonely man's counterpart, his *'vis-à-vis'*. However, the *Catechism* firmly rejects the myth of an aboriginal androgyne. Neither man nor woman are half a creature, and in that sense incomplete, a fragment of humanity. The meaning of 'one for another' lies in the communion of mutual aid possible for those who, as persons, are altogether equal and, precisely because male and female, are complementary. Thus, the existence of distinctive rôles, and even in certain spheres, a primacy or headship for the male, cannot be invoked, by those who would be faithful to the *Catechism*, in order to call in question the more foundational parity of the persons which men and women are.

The mutuality of man and woman must not be regarded as a recipe for what the French call *égoisme à deux*. On the contrary, in a mirroring of its divine archetype the communion between them spills over in two ways. First, through the procreation and nurture of children, it shares in the Creator's own relation to his world. And secondly, as a bearer of stewardship for the sub-human creation, the human pair participate in the provident God's active solicitude for the welfare of his world. The communion between husband and wife leads them not so much to look at each other but, in Antoine de Saint-Exupéry's words, to look together in the same direction.

In many cultures the folk memory carries traces, through myth and ritual, prose and poetry, of a lost golden age. Human life and experience as a declension from glory, a sense that humanity is surrounded by a faded aureole, that human existence is intrinsically related to a dignity: these themes, even without revelation, help to form religion, ethics, literature and even our dreams. 'Be a man! Act like a human being!': these imperatives do not require us to duplicate the flawed actions whereby our species lives but, on the contrary, to remember our original righteousness. They testify to a theological truth, the truth that man was made for Paradise. He was created not only (with the other creatures) good but in such friendship and harmony with his Maker that Adamic glory is only outshone by the radiance of the risen Christ himself. It is a sign of the non-identity of the orders of cultural progress and spiritual life that the most primitive of our forebears – those we call, for want of better names, Man of the Earth (Adam) and Mother of the Living (Eve) – were refulgent with a moral and spiritual splendour not seen again in this planet until Christ. The fourfold harmony of their lives (humankind harmonious with its Maker, man with woman, man at large with the sub-rational world, and each human being within themself) was a music not heard again for millennia on earth.

The difference between man as he is and man as he should be is what we call 'sin'. The full dimensions of that word are not covered by apparently equivalent terms for ethical transgression – 'doing what is wrong'. To call wrong-doing 'sin' is to show an awareness of, in the first instance, the loss of original justice. It is also to affirm that doing the wrong is abuse not only of free will but of the deeper power of self-determination, symptomatised in free will, by which we are called to love God and each other, and so fulfil our nature. Such understanding is revelation-dependent; without it we might well think of what 'sin' connotes as merely faulty growth, psychological debility, the consequence of making mistakes in moral reasoning, or of inadequate social arrangements. Once we have the concept of sin in our grasp, we know that all of these are but scratching the surface. And so the *Catechism* can maintain, strikingly, that Christ must be known as source of grace before Adam is rightly construed as the spring of sin. If the Paraclete, sent by the risen Christ, is to 'convict the world of sin' (John 16:8), this is because he alone can disclose the full distance between the glory we are offered and the falling short we 'achieved'.

The Fall of man, that aboriginal cataclysm whose features, as artists well know, are written on our faces (one need only think of the veridical caricatures of Hieronymus Bosch), is described in Scripture not literally but imagistically.[8] That its reality is not

---

[8] Isabelle Chareire, after ascribing insistence on the 'original' character of sin and of evil to a 'concern to maintain simultaneously the affirmation of the goodness of the Creation and the radicality of fault', points out that, 'if sin is truly original, in the sense that it affects all human existence, humanity cannot designate its commencement', 'Note sur le péché originel dans trois Catéchismes', in *Lumière et Vie* XLIII–1. 216 (1994), pp. 68, 70.

available except via the literary trope of an allegory does not mean, however, that it was not itself an event in time, but only the ongoing condition of humanity. Though all personal sins are renewals of the Fall, on a graduated scale of significance, the Fall itself is not only the foundation of the series but its first member. Before investigating further what it might comprise, it has to be contextualised within a spiritual drama already unfolding before the ensoulment of our first parents. The disruption of the angelic world caused by the refusal of spirits to order their being to a supernatural goal offered freely by God (with all that implies, in terms of the humble acceptance of limitation and even indigence, by these mighty intelligences) profoundly affected the environment in which the first humans were placed. Forms of influence better than human, the holy angels, were counter-balanced with forms worse than human, in the Evil One and *his* angels, a diabolic caricature of the hosts of heaven. The *Catechism* speaks of a general activity of the wicked angels in the world, where a give-away sign is hatred of God and his reign in Jewish Christ. But it also mentions two specific moments of satanic temptation: the attempt to prize Jesus away from his mission (the Temptations in the Wilderness), which failed, and the 'type' to which that christological mystery stands as 'antitype' – the seduction of man from the way of obedience to the good purposes of his Creator, which succeeded. Why God permits the Evil One so to act is a theological mystery (the purest case of the problem of evil, in fact), but the mystery of Satan is, if not illuminated, then epistemically bounded by the mystery of hope whereby, as the Letter to the Romans has it (8:28), 'we know that in everything God works for good with those who love him'.

The Fall of man, as the *Catechism* describes it, is the loss of a friendship with God whose condition was the only one worthy of the dignity of a spiritual creature – namely, free obedience to the Creator. The 'tree of the knowledge of good and evil' in the parable of Eden represents the difference between the Creator, whose knowledge of good and evil is their very constitution as such, and the creature who finds his own identity through acquiescence in the really good, rather than through the self-styled and spurious 'creativity' which would spin the laws of its being from out of its own substance. Revelation does not tell us in what *genre* of human action the Fall occurred. It does more. It shows us its cankered heart. As the matrix of the personal sins of the future, the sin of the Fall stamps a family-resemblance on its offspring. Whatever the sins of men may be, they always show two inter-connected features – disobedience to God and a lack of trust in his Fatherly goodness.

With the Fall the divine relationship, and man's own relation with himself, are damaged, apparently irreparably. First, by rejecting the principled freedom with which he came to consciousness in favour of an autarchy without grounding in the good, the human animal lost its original holiness, and the destiny of participation in the divine life which the Father had willed for it. In the acute formulation of the seventh century Byzantine theologian St Maximus the Confessor, man chose to be 'like God' – which paradoxically, was, *toutes proportions gardées*, exactly what God had intended for him – but 'like God' '*without God, and in opposition to God, not according to God*'. Thus estranged from God, the history of false conceptualisation of the divine begins. The guilty fear with which newly fallen humanity regarded God generated the idolatrous image of a God jealous of his own prerogatives – a caricature of the true Father of both Christian and Adamic revelation. Secondly, man now faced the consequences of choosing to ignore his own creaturely condition and thus his proper good. A multiple disharmony invaded his being. The disintegration of the inner unity of his faculties and powers, harmonised as these had been by original justice, fostered tension between body and soul, between male and female human beings, between man himself and the rest of the creation. Finally, with sin came death. A biological ending to the human organism there would always have been, but the sense of that ending was meant to be a felicitous transition to transfigured life in God. Death as the abiding separation of body and soul, what Newman's Gerontius called

> the emptying out of each constituent and natural force by which I come to be[9]

---

[9] J. H. Newman, *The Dream of Gerontius* (London 1866).

is the sign and seal of the interior collapse of the human microcosm. Death is sin's sacrament. And as death spares no man, so sin is universally pervasive in the human story.

An understanding of human history as poised between two Adams, each of which has affected mankind for evil or good, is particularly indebted to Paul's Letter to the Romans. The Church has grasped the dramatic symbolism of the two humanities, Adam's and Christ's, as making an ontological claim. The sea, both inner and outer, of human misery is not to be understood, nor is the self-destructive impulse towards evil to be interpreted aright, without a recognition of the Fall of human nature in its prototype. This doctrine – that all human beings fell in Adam, since through his sin the nature for which he bore responsibility as its primal head was transmitted to us as he had left it – is often derided nowadays as anti-humane. On the contrary, the acceptance of a historic Fall which has wounded each of us in our inmost constitution, is a vital safeguard for human sanity. It saves us from the moralistic titanism of belief in the possibility of our self-perfecting, a perfectionism which is peculiarly pernicious when set to work, in the form of social and ideological cleansing, by the Guardians of the State. As the *Catechism* itself points out, not to know that man has a damaged constitution leads to many errors of judgment in such realms as education and customs, politics and social action. This dogma also strips us of the pride with which the morally respectable are prone to view the ethically down-at-heel. The Marquis de Sade and myself are brothers.

The doctrine of original sin is not, however, an invitation to wallow in irrational guilt. As the text makes clear, the term 'sin' here is used analogically: there can be no sin in the basic and primary sense of that word where personal wrong-doing is absent – as it is in the newly-born. Nor should it be taken to imply, in the manner of Jansenius and Luther, that human nature is now a rotting hulk, or a cesspit even whose sweet exhalations – our apparently virtuous deeds – are actually foetid without grace. We are talking about a human nature wounded, not a humanity de-natured. The image of God persists though covered, as the Fathers stressed, in grime.

Nor again, finally, should a classical representation of the doctrine, such as is found in the *Catechism's* pages, be taken to exclude altogether that more sociological understanding of the 'sin of the world' which the Baptist, in St John's Gospel, described the Lamb of God as 'taking away' (John 1:29). The human sins which replicate the Fall and build up the ant-heap of busyness in evil which it started, naturally leave behind 'structures' and 'situations' in the human city where a sinfulness which is no individual's responsibility takes public form.

In the drama of the conflict between good and evil which has thus passed from the city of the angels to the city of man, God has not abandoned this divided protagonist which is ourselves. In the very account of the Fall in Genesis, the sacred authors strike the different note of the 'Proto-Gospel' – the divine promise of a redemption which will bring to a triumphant conclusion the struggle between the Evil One and the woman who, though once complicitous with evil, remained mother of all the living (Genesis 3:15). And here the *Catechism* prepares to turn to the subject of the *Son*, for, as it relates, Tradition has found in the Jesus Christ obedient to the Father unto death the perfect Fulfiller of Adam's project, with a human Mother graced, in view of his work, by the constancy lacking in Eve. God permitted the Fall of humanity so that the extremity of his love for man might be revealed in so great a Redeemer (Paragraphs 411, 412).

V

*Professing the Faith: The Creed on the Son**

Unusually for the work we are reviewing, the authors of the *Catechism* incorporate into the opening of their christological survey a warm, personal statement of confession which appeals to the activity of Father and Spirit in bringing about their (and the Church's) fundamental appreciation of Jesus Christ. 'Moved by the grace of the Holy Spirit and drawn by the Father, *we* believe in Jesus and confess ...'.[1] There follows St Peter's profession of faith at Caesarea Philippi (Matthew 16:16) that Jesus is not only Christ but Son of the living God: the first papal *credo* on which 'Christ built his Church'.

The opening paragraphs of the *Catechism's* treatment of Jesus Christ define the Gospel, the Good News of Christianity, by the Incarnational formula, 'God has sent his Son'. The message of Jesus, after all, during his earthly ministry, concerned both the Giver of the Kingdom (the Father) and its Bringer (the Son). Only so can we make sense of the summary of Jesus' preaching of the Gospel in St Mark 'The time is fulfilled, and the Kingdom of God is at hand' (Mark 1:15). The Gospel of Jesus Christ in the subjective genitive, the Gospel that was his, is identically the Gospel of Jesus Christ in the objective genitive, the Gospel that he is (Mark 1:1). St Paul, in formulating for the Christians of Galatia what it was that characterised the climax

---

* = *Catechism*, Paragraphs 422–679.
[1] Paragraph 424, italics added.

of history his contemporaries had just lived through, could find no better words than those with which the entire Christology of the *Catechism* opens: 'When the time had fully come, God sent forth his Son, born of woman, born under the law, to redeem those who were under the law, so that we might receive adoption as sons' (Galatians 4:4–5). And in a deliberately uncomfortable juxtaposition of the language of time with that of eternity, the *Catechism* proclaims Jesus the Jew – 'Jesus of Nazareth, born a Jew of a daughter of Israel at Bethlehem at the time of King Herod the Great and the emperor Caesar Augustus, a carpenter by trade, who died crucified in Jerusalem under the procurator Pontius Pilate during the reign of the emperor Tiberius' – as none other than the 'eternal Son of God made man', who 'came from God' (John 13:3), 'descended from heaven' (John 3:13; 6:33), 'came in the flesh' (I John 4:2).[2]

Some remarks by authors both new and old may help us to appreciate why, in a few lines of prose, the *Catechism* twice adopts a formula of deliberate self-engagement: 'We believe and confess'. A recent theological meditation on the mystery of Christ by the Hungarian Cistercian Roch Kereszty has usefully reminded its readers that the assimilation of Christology, the truth about Jesus, presupposes spiritual life in the root meaning of that phrase – life in the Holy Spirit, just as, in turn, the nourishment a solid Christology provides should enable one to lead that spiritual life more consciously, more intensely.[3] The interpretation of the career of Jesus Christ depends in part, therefore, on the student's openness to the working of the Spirit of Christ, who promised to recall to the disciples' minds all that Jesus did and taught. This being so, it must also turn on one's attitude to the initiatives, actual and possible, of the Father, who is the Source of both Son and Spirit. Insofar as there is a crisis of doctrine in modern theology (something more acute, certainly, in Anglicanism than in

[2] Paragraph 423.
[3] R. A. Kereszty, O. Cist., *Jesus Christ. Fundamentals of Christology* (Staten Island, New York, 1991), p. xvii. Kereszty's explanation for this state of affairs is that 'It is Christ himself present in the believer through his Spirit who guarantees his own reality to the believer and helps him understand the implications of his mystery', ibid.

Catholicism), this is surely because many Christians have not experienced, through faith and conversion, the 'reality of what the traditional doctrines proclaim'.[4] Pope Leo the Great, in his sermons on the Ascension, declares that faith, in order to be 'nobler and firmer', is now grounded 'not on sight but on doctrine', but he immediately adds that 'the hearts of those who believe follow this doctrine by a light that comes from above'.[5] The *Catechism*, like these authors, is drawing attention to the transformed awareness with which the student must approach the Gospels if he or she is to do so theologically rather than archaeologically. The historical method, set to work in a neutral fashion, can take us a certain way, but only the gift of faith, given meat to bite on by the materials of Tradition, can enable us to continue down the path of christological understanding to journey's end. (Thus fortified, the believing historian can then, of course, return to his task with an ampler concept of its true dimensions, drawing from the Church's faith illuminating hypotheses about the generally available data – and this is what the Catholic exegete should be doing.)

The loving knowledge of Jesus Christ has to be the centre of all catechesis – not only because in him the entire divine plan of salvation holds together, as Pope John Paul II's apostolic exhortation *Catechesi tradendae* had already remarked in its fifth paragraph, but also because all the dimensions of Christian existence, in suffering and glory, are pre-contained in him, as the wonderful peroration of Paul's Letter to the Philippians (3:7–11) makes clear. Not only should such a knowing love of Christ lead ineluctably – 'irresistibly'[6] – to evangelisation; it also finds natural expression in the felt need to learn more about the faith whose centre he is. The *Catechism* proposes to satisfy this need (though of course its teaching is above all a *point de départ* for lifelong reflection and further study) firstly by an exposition of what is involved in the christological titles used by the Creed – 'Christ', 'Son of God', 'Lord', and secondly

---

[4] T. Weinandy, O.F.M. Cap., 'Maurice Wiles and Christian Doctrine', *New Blackfriars* 75. 880 (1994), p. 169.
[5] Leo the Great, *Sermons* 2, 2.
[6] Paragraph 429.

by investigation of those principal events in the life of Christ (his 'cardinal works', as the mediaeval theologian Arnold of Bounival called them) which the Gospels depict and the liturgies of the Church both celebrate and explore.

To set out the faith of the Church about the divine Son by way of christological titles is to hark back to a favoured approach of the Fathers. Origen, for instance, in his commentary on the Gospel of John, treats the titles as manifestations of different aspects of the single yet complex mystery which is the God-man. It is also to pick up a popular theme in the high scholarship of twentieth century New Testament study. Notice, however, that the *Catechism* does not undertake an exhaustive catalogue of such titles (which would have to include, for instance, the much-discussed 'Son of Man' and, less controversially, 'The Holy One of God'), but concentrates on what it calls the 'chief' titles – identified as such precisely by their naming in the ecumenical Creed.

The titles tell us who it is that the New Testament *names*. They are fittingly preceded, therefore, by an account of *the* 'Holy Name', *Jesus*. Used sparingly in public discourse by an older generation of Catholics from the same concern with reverence which led the Jews of Jesus' time to restrict the pronouncing of the tetragrammaton *YHWH* to a once-yearly festal moment – on the Day of Atonement, by the high priest in the Holy of Holies of the Jerusalem Temple – and acknowledged in the Liturgy by a slight bowing of the head, the Name of Jesus is 'holy' because, in the *Catechism's* words, it signifies that 'the very name of God [in biblical thinking, his *reality*] is present in the person of his Son, made man for the universal and definitive redemption from sins' (Paragraph 432). For the name 'Jesus' – Jeshua – means 'God saves'. If the Psalmist can cry out to 'the God of our salvation', 'deliver us, and forgive us our sins, for thy name's sake' (79:9), then through the Incarnation the divine Name in question has been united with the humanity of us all, with the inevitable result that

> there is salvation in no one else, for there is no other name under heaven given among men by which we must be saved

– thus St Peter's testimony to the Sanhedrin in the Acts of the Apostles (4:12). The name which, during the public ministry, was feared by demons, and, among the disciples, enabled them to work wonderful deeds, and to ask of the Father with confidence, was 'glorified' by the Resurrection of the Son made man. In a specifically *Paschal* theology of the Name, the *Catechism* understands the Resurrection here, by reference to the Philippians hymn (2:9–10), as the Father's empowering of the Name of Jesus, which henceforth will manifest in its fullness the power to bring creation to fulfilment which attaches to the 'Name which is above every name', that of the uncreated divinity. Aware, no doubt, of the rich development of liturgical devotion to the Name of Jesus in the Western Middle Ages (with which Dominicans were particularly associated),[7] as of the Eastern Christian 'Jesus Prayer', to which they explicitly allude,[8] the authors of the *Catechism* call the holy Name 'the centre of Christian prayer'. The *Hail Mary* culminates in a prayer of praise of 'the fruit of thy womb, Jesus', and if its second half, the *Holy Mary*, seeks Mary's assistance 'at the hour of our death', this prayer of petition may find its answer in the grace of dying with the Name of Jesus on one's lips, as have many saints, such as, the *Catechism* recalls, St Joan of Arc.

The title 'Christ' means both the Messiah of Israel's hope but also something more. In Israel, kings, priests and, less frequently, prophets were anointed as a sign of a divine mission with which they were thus entrusted. To call Jesus 'the Anointed One', *ho christos, par excellence* is to say that he perfectly fulfilled a divine mission signalised, but not exhaustively defined, by the Old Testament concept of Messiahship.

Following hints in some early ecclesiastical writers, and notably Eusebius of Caesarea, the Catholic theology of the last hundred years has accepted an analysis of the work of Christ in terms of three 'offices' – royal, priestly and prophetic – first

---

[7]R. P. Biasiotto, *History of the Development of Devotion to the Holy Name* (New York 1943); see also R. W. Pfaff, *New Liturgical Feasts in Later Mediaeval England* (Oxford 1970).

[8]On this, see: A Monk of the Eastern Church [L. Gillet], *On the Invocation of the Name of Jesus* (London 1948).

worked out in systematic form by divines of the Reformed and Lutheran traditions. Exploiting texts from Isaiah and Zechariah, the *Catechism* speaks of all three rôles as properly messianic, for the Messiah's activity could be understood in each of these three ways. Although there is reason to think that the Mother of Jesus may herself have been a Davidide, the requirement, arising from the engraced understanding of the divine will by Jewish prophetism, that the Messiah will be of David's house and line is met, for the New Testament, by Joseph's legal adoption of Mary's child. (In Jewish society, sonship was primarily legal, not biological.)

But in any case, for the *Catechism*, which seeks support here from the Trinitarian theology of Irenaeus, the making of the messianic mission of Jesus is done in the 'anointing' of his humanity with the Holy Spirit at the first moment of his conception, and even in his eternal being as the Son, since everlastingly his existence has been suffused with the Holy Spirit, the unitive personal Bond of Father and Son. In this sense his messianic consecration took place in eternity; it is revealed in time when he was baptised by John. Then it was that, in the words of Peter to the household of Cornelius 'God anointed Jesus of Nazareth with the Holy Spirit and with power' (Acts 10:38). As is well known, Jesus showed reserve about the public dissemination of his messianic claim, owing to the wide credence currently given to an excessively humanistic, and basically, political, interpretation of the Messiah's task. With the confession of Peter at Caesarea Philippi, however, Jesus' confidence in the inevitability and even imminence of his Passion enabled him to have done with all equivocation. He was to be a Messiah of the Cross, and so beyond all politically-liberationist misunderstanding. The *Catechism* speaks of him as disclosing the authentic content of his messianic regality under two related figures: that of the Son of Man come down from heaven, with a transcendent, then, not this-worldly identity, and that of the Suffering Servant of the Deutero-Isaianic oracles with a mission to bear the transgressions of many. The true meaning of Christ's kingship is thus given only from the Cross, where, as in much Christian iconography, he reigns in glory. If, with the Anglo-Saxon poem *The Dream of the Rood*, the

Catechism portrays the tree of Calvary as diademed, it reserves the open proclamation of Christ the King for the period after the Resurrection when the Father enthrones Jesus as Lord and Christ.

The title 'Son of God' is expanded by the Creed, in line with the theophany accounts of the Gospels for the Baptism and Transfiguration of Christ, through a reference to the *only-begotten* character of Jesus' divine Sonship. The *Catechism* distinguishes between, on the one hand, an honorific, 'adoptive', divine sonship, which the Hebrew Bible felt able to ascribe to a great variety of creatures, from angels to men, from the children of Israel as a whole to their king in particular, and, on the other hand, what it terms 'transcendent' filiation. The exegetical foundation for this distinction lies partly in the way certain affirmations of Jesus' sonship are ascribed by the New Testament not to human inference ('flesh and blood') but to divine revelation ('my Father who is in heaven'). This privileged class is evidence, accordingly, for a non-adoptive – which can only mean ontologically divine, and thus 'transcendent' – filiation. Then again there is the curious fact that the messianic claim Jesus at last allowed himself at his trial should have been termed blasphemous: it was as a messianic pretender who claimed to share in the divine attributes that he was condemned. Consonant with this suggestion is the linguistic oddity whereby, in speaking with the disciples, Jesus was always careful to refer to 'my Father and your Father'. 'Our Father' was what he told the disciples to say, not what he said with them. He understood himself to be Son absolutely or unconditionally – and therefore uniquely. Only after the Resurrection does Christ's divine sonship appear more manifestly in the power of his exalted humanity – thus enabling the apostolic community to confess how they had seen the glory that is his as only Son of the Father, full of grace and truth (John 1:14).

The last of the titles common to both Creed and Scriptures is 'Lord' – like Son of God, a designation capable of infinite gradation from a respectful doffing of the cap ('Sir') at one end of a spectrum to adoring acknowledgment of the world's Maker at the other. The *Catechism* distinguishes between a usage that signifies veneration and trust, on the one hand, and one that, in dependence on the action of the Holy Spirit moving a person interiorly, recognises the divine mystery in Jesus. And if it ascribes the first of these to Matthew's account of the ministry, and the second to Luke's narratives of the childhood of Christ, it reserves to the Gospel of John not only the use of the term to acknowledge the Son's Godhead (20:28), but also the first example of the warm, intimate connotations which this title would take on in the future (21:12, compare 'our Lord', 'our blessed Lord' – common dominical designations in Catholic parlance). Still, 'our very human Lord' – the phrase belongs to mediaeval devotional life – is also the dread Judge of the Romanesque tympana. The *Catechism* does not forget that the application to Jesus of this divine Name of the Septuagint translation of the Hebrew Bible brings in its train such attributes as power, glory, honour – all of which the Father manifests through the Son in raising him from the dead. Christ's Lordship over nature and history implicitly denies the justice of all earthly claims to dominion over freedom in its deepest personal sense. To affirm that 'Jesus is Lord' is to cry ruin on all totalitarian systems and ideologies. And if Jesus Christ our Lord is thus the key to human history, he must be not its centre only but also its end. Appropriately, then, the meditation on the titles is rounded off by a reminder of the eschatological invocation of this same Lord – *Maran atha*, 'May the Lord come!' (I Corinthians 16:22; cf. Apocalypse 22:20).

Although the *Catechism* proposes to turn immediately after its exposition of the christological titles to the christological mysteries – that more characteristically mediaeval and early modern way of practising reflection on the Word made flesh – its account of the Conception and Birth of Christ is better described as setting forth the ontological pre-conditions of the story unfolded in the mysteries of Christ's life. Resuming the self-committing tone which distinguishes the preamble to the *Catechism's* Christology, its makers 'confess' with the Fathers of the Nicene and Constantinopolitan synods that the Word consubstantial with the Father 'for us men and for our salvation ... came down from heaven; by the power of the Holy Spirit he became incarnate from the Virgin Mary, and was made man'. And here we launch straightaway into the *motives* of the Incarnation (Paragraphs 456–60).

The *Catechism* enumerates four. The first concentrates on man's damaged nature and guilty actions. The fourth century Greek Father Gregory of Nyssa, now cited, speaks of human nature after the Fall as plangently as any modern Existentialist (our nature was in need of healing, raising, resuscitation). There is reason enough here for the hominisation of the Word, so that God might save us by reconciling us with himself. But secondly – and complementarily, for the First Letter of St John illustrates both approaches – the Word became flesh so that we might know the love of God. Both here and in the following two 'motives' suggested, human sinfulness need not be presupposed. As in the famous late mediaeval debate between Thomists and Scotists, the Word, arguably, might have assumed humanity even had there been no Fall. The further revelation of the divine life, and the transfiguration of humankind by a deeper union therewith, would be its own justification. The two remaining rationales for the Incarnation spell out the moral and mystical implications, respectively, of the disclosure of the divine nature, and of the communion of the divine persons, in Jesus Christ. First, the Word was made flesh to become our model of holiness: the *Catechism* calls Christ, in terms the Antiochene theology of the patristic age would have relished, the model of the Beatitudes and the norm of the new law of charity. Then secondly, and picking up the emphasis of the other chief school of christological thought among the Fathers – that of Alexandria – it speaks of the eternal Son assuming our humanity so that we might become sharers in the divine nature. This theme of our divinisation through Christ, sometimes considered exclusively Oriental and even Eastern Orthodox, rather than Western and Catholic, is illustrated by telling citations not only from such Greek Fathers as Irenaeus and Athanasius but also from the classical theologian of the Latin tradition, Thomas Aquinas.

To those who would consider Incarnational believing as simply one possible version of Christology to set alongside others the *Catechism* retorts that, on the contrary, it is the distinctive sign of Christian faith: in the words of First Timothy the 'great ... mystery of our religion' (3:16). The first seven Ecumenical Councils of the Church (and the lesser synods which prepared and commented them) unfolded little by little this basic datum of the apostolic faith that Jesus, while true man, is also one with the Father as his Word. The *Catechism* treats its readers to a miniature history of the conciliar Christology in its development, though the great story is slightly dislocated in its telling by a decision to regard it as two overlapping narratives – one concerned with the coincidence of divinity and humanity in the person of Christ, and the other more preoccupied with how One who was God might also be fully human, without impairment of that humanity. If the Council of Antioch (284) defined against the heresiarch Paul of Samosata that Jesus is Son of God by nature, not adoption, the First Ecumenical Council, Nicaea I, in 325 anathematised the teaching of Arius that he came out of nothing (as creatures do) and thus was of another substance than the Father. (Here the *Catechism* might have added, for the sake of symmetry in its conciliar references, that the relevant clauses of the Nicene faith were solemnly reiterated, and embodied in the final version of the ecumenical Creed, at the Second Ecumenical Council, Constantinople I, in 381.) Not all, however, was pellucid yet. While Nestorius saw in Christ a human person conjoined with the divine person of the Son of God, St Cyril of Alexandria persuaded the Third Ecumenical Council, Ephesus, in 431, that there is no other subject of Christ's humanity than the person of the divine Son who assumed it in making it his own. The Fourth Ecumenical Council, Chalcedon, in 451, taught that in the single hypostasis (underlying subject, and thus, for beings endowed with spiritual activity, *person*) of our Lord Jesus Christ the two natures are united inseparably but without confusion, while the Fifth Ecumenical, Constantinople II, meeting in 553, cleared up a possible ambiguity in the text of Chalcedon by insisting that this single hypostasis was indeed that of one of the Holy Trinity – who was, therefore, the subject of (even) Christ's sufferings and death. With this 'Neo-Chalcedonian' conviction thus integrated into the public doctrine of the Church, it was safe enough at the Sixth of the Councils, Constantinople III, in 691, to speak freely of a duality

Professing the Faith: The Creed on the Son 61

of wills in the Redeemer, such that he chose in a properly human fashion to do, in his loving service of the Father as man all that, as the divine Word, co-responsive with the Spirit to the Father, he had willed as God from all eternity. Finally, at the Seventh Ecumenical Council, Nicea II, 787, the union of divinity and humanity in Christ was pronounced so close that veneration of the painterly image of the body of Jesus can count as homage to the uncreated person of the Son.

The *Catechism* affirms resoundingly enough the reality in Jesus of all those anthropological elements – soul, mind, will, heart, as well as body – that make up human nature in its totality. It allows itself more space for the topic of the human knowledge of One in whom human nature and divine were held together in his own person. On the one hand, the human mind of the Lord entertained its knowledge in a properly human way, which could not mean an unlimited way. And here it seems appropriate to make mention of the cumulative character of Jesus' understanding as also of the way much of it must have been acquired – like our own – through experience. On the other hand, the union of the soul of Jesus with the divine Word made possible to him a source of understanding not available to us – and we see the fruits thereof in his intimate and immediate knowledge of the Father. In the same basket may be placed also his penetrating insight into the secrets of the human heart, and – crucial to his redemptive mission – his grasp of the saving plan of God and the part he was to play in its realisation. Although the authors of the *Catechism* do not broach the question of *how* divine knowledge was thus infused into Jesus' human intelligence, the conditions under which his human mind could apprehend what was in his divine mind may be thought of as analogous to those regulating the process of translation from one language to another. As the divine person of the Son, Jesus was continuously in possession of the divine knowledge which is an inherent attribute of the Godhead (and distinct from the divine nature itself less in reality than in our apprehension). As completely man, he had a human mind subject to all the limitations in which human nature is involved. We should expect that, as Jesus 'grew in wisdom' (Luke 2:52), this human mind would itself grow in its capacity to draw on the divine mind, going from strength to strength in intellectual power *pari passu* with the development of Jesus' human holiness in moral force (the 'grace' also mentioned by the same Lucan text just cited), as it passed from one immaculate stage of life to another further advanced still – until finally, in the Cross and Resurrection, his human mind and will attained a total transparency to the divine mind and will possessed by the Son, from the Father, in the Spirit. Of that condition the Heart of Jesus, as venerated in the cult of the 'Sacred Heart', is the primary symbol, for the heart, in biblical anthropology, is the deep source of acts at once of understanding and of will. Appropriately, then, the *Catechism* makes its own words of Pope Pius XII on the Heart of the Lord as the revelation of his love unto death both of the Father and of all human beings.

The Creed maintains of the eternal Son that he was in time 'conceived by the power of the Holy Spirit and born of the Virgin Mary'. While for Catholicism, Mariology is founded on Christology (and ecclesiology – but the *Catechism* in accordance with the structure of the Creed itself, defers consideration of this until it speaks of the Holy Spirit in his own person), nevertheless Christology can itself be illuminated by Mariology. The Mother can throw light on her Son, as once she brought him into earthly light's domain. The glories of Mary relevant to the Conception and Birth of the Son made man – her predestination, original righteousness, and virgin motherhood – have to do with the sovereign initiative of the Father in bringing to completion his promises to the human race, and the preparation in Israel of the 'fullness of time' (Galatians 4:4). That moment – the Annunciation made to Mary – is 'plenary', filled with unsurpassable content, because in it the Creator begins to relate to the world in a new way, as its Redeemer, becoming as he does so, without derogation from his deity, one of his own creatures.

It is sometimes said – by, for instance, the contemporary Eastern Orthodox – that the dogma of Mary's Immaculate Conception cuts off the Mother of the Redeemer from the people of Israel of whom, as the Daughter of Zion *par excellence*, she should be the symbol. The *Catechism* carefully avoids any such impression by treating the Immaculate Conception only after it has spoken of Mary's predestination – something which it sees working itself out through the history of the Elder Covenant. In particular, Mary is the culmination of the series of holy women who stud the pages of the Hebrew Bible like stars. And just as, in the Old Testament, the more charged with significance election is, the more interior it becomes, so now, in Mary's conception, the grace of the Old Covenant reaches its point of maximum penetration by enabling the entire constitution of one Jewess to be transformed by God.

The Immaculate Conception means that, from the first moment of her existence Mary was wholly sustained by the sanctifying grace of God so that she could fully give her responsive 'Yes' to the extraordinary vocation made known to her, and (we may add) live out that vocation to the end. This was, in the argumentation supplied by the mediaeval Franciscan Blessed Duns Scotus (drawn on in the definition of this dogma by Pope Pius IX) the *praeredemptio*: Mary's redemption by anticipation of the Saviour's triumph. The *Catechism* admits – not grudgingly, but with a glorying in the fact – that the various traditions of the Church, Eastern and Western, have found different idioms in which to express Mary's original righteousness. The Byzantines speak of her all-holiness; such early Latin doctors as Peter Chrysologus and Maximus of Turin of how she was betrothed to God from her mother's womb, and made the Lord's worthy receptacle by 'original grace'. As the holy and immaculate Spouse of the Father she foreshadows the mystery of the Church as the Bride of Christ, spoken of by the Writer to the Ephesians (1:4), for Mary is the image of redeemed humanity's final condition, when there will be no more sorrow for sin, and men and women will be at last entirely free.

The *Catechism* celebrates Mary's Annunciation as the most wonderful example of the 'obedience of faith' described by Paul in Romans (1:5) as the essence of the Christian life. Hers was a total gift of self to the divine plan of salvation with (thanks to sinlessness) nothing held back. And, citing Irenaeus – a favoured witness in the *Catechism's* soteriology – she become, by a reversal of Eve's act of disobedience, the cause of salvation both for herself and for the whole human race. One thinks of St Bernard's evocation of the moment of the Annunciation:

when the angel speaks, all Israel, all humankind, all creation wait breathlessly for Mary's reply. St Thomas, too, speaks of the Virgin's consent as sought in lieu of that of human nature as a whole.

At the Annunciation, the Spirit comes upon Mary just as in all eternity he had rested on the Son. As a result the humanity of the Logos, taken from Mary, was fitted for, and corresponded to, the being of the Word himself. The *Catechism* devotes its remaining paragraphs on Mary at this juncture to her divine virgin-motherhood. While serenely confessing, with the *Catholica* of all times and places, the virginity of Mary, an apologia is offered by way of defence of this doctrine against those who regard its New Testament basis as legendary expansion of a more primitive Gospel tradition. Matthew and Luke would simply have been fashioning a rod for their own backs – as was soon shown by the experience of apologists like Justin and Origen in defending the faith to Jews and Gentiles respectively. It could be added that, given the prominence of fathers in the birth-narratives of Scripture (as in social reality), the consequent marginalising of Joseph is hard to explain save by invoking the pressure of reality. It has been the increasingly underscored faith-conviction of the Church that this virginity of Mary's is perpetual: the 'brothers of Jesus', such as James and Joseph, can be identified as children of that 'other Mary' (Matthew 28:1) whom early writers identify as the sister-in-law of Joseph, wife to Clopas. What the Liturgy celebrates, in calling Mary 'ever virgin', Catholic divinity explores further in treating any supposed extended physical family of Mary as a confusing irrelevance to her central rôle in the community of the Messiah, which is to be the spiritual mother of his many brethren.

The virginal conception of Jesus may be defended not only in its historicity, but also in its divine rationale. It manifests, as the *Catechism* points out, the 'absolute initiative' of God[9] – and does so in a stupendous and unmistakeable fashion, which is why so many rebel against this doctrine. Just as sexual generation brings before our conceptual eye man as willing, achieving, creating – and, consequently, is profoundly unsuited to be the

---

[9]Paragraph 503.

expression of the redemptive Incarnation, which depends on the grace of God alone, so virginity, by contrast, sums up the helplessness of human beings in the face of God's sovereign grace. Our human nature, as such, cannot contribute anything to the coming of the divine Word, now personally enfleshed, into the created world. Moreover, the innovatory character of this human beginning well expresses the twofold newness of the Covenant which Christ will inaugurate in his person, and in his blood. He is the new Adam, initiating a new humanity; and the bringer of a new birth for all those who, regenerated by faith, will be his brothers and sisters, the adopted sons and daughters of the Father.

Two further considerations can be adduced, one concerned with the basic God-man relationship and the other with its concrete actualisation as the Church. Mary's virginity, embodying as this does a total self-donation with all her powers to God, is perfectly suited to be the sign of authentic faith which likewise entails a complete spiritual openness to him. And this is true above all of the climatic phase of the divine economy begun by the Flesh-taking of the Word, which is nothing less, as we have seen, than a re-creation of humanity. Furthermore, the Church, which is the continuing form of the Word Incarnate's saving activity in the world, is hailed in Tradition as virgin and mother: she keeps herself intact in faith for her Bridegroom, Jesus Christ, and brings forth children by her preaching and the sacrament of baptismal regeneration. In this kind of symbolic thought, it is only appropriate that the Church's being should be summed up in advance in its paradigm, blessed Mary, a virgin mother in the flesh as well as in the spirit. In these two final suggestions as to why it was fitting that the Word should be virginally conceived, the *Catechism* makes good the weaknesses of an exclusive emphasis, in the spirit of the great Protestant dogmatician Karl Barth, on the incapacity of human nature to contribute anything to the incarnating God. Thanks to the Word she conceived in her heart Mary *did* contribute, on humanity's behalf, a response that was both dedicated or virginal, and productive, or motherly: *her* gift, though one based, certainly, on grace, to the Redeemer to be conceived in her womb.

We turn now to the mysteries of the life of Christ, the principal form in which – at least in terms of bulk – the *Catechism* presents its Christology. It opens by pointing out that the Creed, in speaking only of the beginning and end of the life of the Lord Jesus (Conception and Birth on the one hand, Death and Resurrection on the other) did not intend to marginalise the mysteries of the centre (the 'hidden' life of Jesus, and the events of the public ministry), but to illuminate them. The presupposition is that the entire life-story of Jesus should be seen as a revelatory sign of salvation, a disclosure of the mystery of God in his plan to bring true welfare – healing and wholeness – to humankind. While his life has its high points and decisive moments, each of these shares in the mystery of that life as an entirety, and so, in the last resort, can be validly understood only from out of that fullness. Here the *Catechism* confesses its own inadequacy: catechesis must round out the portrait of these great dramatic *tableaux* of the Gospels – though it can never round them off, for their significance, as presentations of the Infinite translucent in the finite, is inexhaustible. What was visible in the scenes of his earthly life leads back into the invisible mystery of the Son's eternal procession from the Father, and its continuation in his redemptive mission to the world. In the *Catechism's* own preferred terminology, the mysteries of Christ have three features in common: they are revelatory, redemptive, recapitulatory. The events of the life of Jesus are *revelatory*: they disclose the Father and his will; they are *redemptive*: they repair the torn fabric of human living and make expiation for its criminous aspects; they are *recapitulatory*: they re-establish fallen man in his aboriginal, Adamic vocation (Paragraphs 516–18).

At the same time, because Christ lived his life not for himself but for us, and both acts and suffers as our model, it is only fitting that we participate in these mysteries ourselves. As Son of God, and mighty Victor over sin and death, he has the power to make possible what is thus proper. By annulling the distance which separates us from him he enables us to live in him, and him in us. A particularly fine statement of what the *Catechism* has in mind here can be found in Dom Columba Marmion's early twentieth century classic *Christ in his Mysteries*, which integrates biblical, patristic and liturgical materials into its account of the mysteries of the life of Christ in much the same sort of way as the text we are studying.[10] Marmion declares that Christ's mysteries are our mysteries for three reasons – because he lived them for us; because he shows himself to us in them as our model; and because in those mysteries, he 'makes but one with us', uniting himself with his own, and meriting grace for us by them. Here both the thought and its expression foreshadow the *Catechism's* so strikingly that it is difficult to think the resemblances are chance. What is not borrowed from Marmion is his fundamental theological explanation of the continuing power of the mysteries of Christ's earthly life, which turns on a distinction between the events and their 'virtue', as well as on the high priestly heavenly intercession of the Saviour. Here the *Catechism* prefers to turn to the seventeenth century French School of spiritual theology, as represented by a passage from St John Eudes' *Tractatus de regno Jesu*, where the matter is left more simply as the voluntary disposition of the divine Son:

> for it is the plan of the Son of God to make us and the whole Church partake in his mysteries and to extend them to and continue them in us and in his whole Church.

The mysteries of the infancy of Christ and those of his hidden life at Nazareth are considered together, and both sets are prefaced by a brief account of the preparation of the first 'advent' or coming of the Lord, which gives its name to the pre-Christmas liturgical season of the Latin Church. What the Jewish prophets, in a variety of ways, foretold, pagans obscurely sensed – a reference chiefly relating, no doubt, to the prophecy of a golden Child in Vergil's *Fourth Eclogue*, though the rôle of salvational mediator figures in the mystery religions popular in the Greco-Roman world around the time of Christ may also be in mind. The *Catechism* deals swiftly with the Precursor and Baptist John: a figure of whom more might be made, given his

---

[10] C. Marmion, O.S.B., *Christ in his Mysteries* (E.t. London and Glasgow 1925).

pivotal rôle in both mediaeval Western and contemporary Eastern Christian spirituality. In modern Catholic theology Hans Urs von Balthasar has treated John the Baptist as a structuring figure of the Gospel, while Jean Daniélou spoke of his continuing presence and activity, in the communion of saints, wherever sinners come through the acceptance of judgment to repentance. Here the Gospel allusions to John are collected in a christological spirit, treating him exclusively as witness to Christ as the Lamb of God: quite intelligible at this point in the *Catechism's déroulement.*

The mystery of Christmas arouses in the authors a Franciscan spirit: they emphasise the poverty of the circumstances of this birth – in which they see 'heaven's glory'.[11] Surprisingly, of the two pieces of liturgical poetry they select to illustrate how the Church 'sings unceasingly in glorification of this night', it is the Latin antiphon rather than the Byzantine kontakion which is the more austerely metaphysical, praising the Nativity for the 'wonderful exchange' it brought about, as God appears in man's nature so as to clothe humanity with his own. The kontakion, from the seventh century poet Romanos the Melodist, conjures up the atmosphere of the crib, though poet and theologian in Romanos conspire to great effect when he speaks of the earth as providing a grotto – the cave of Bethlehem – for the Inaccessible One. The image puts not only memorably but into a soteriological context (that of access to the Inaccessible) the truth that at Christmas the eternal God became a little child.

The mysteries of the childhood of Christ are four: the Circumcision, the Epiphany, the Presentation in the Temple, and the Flight into Egypt (together with the Massacre of the Innocents). Rightly, the *Catechism* supposes that what the Church celebrates liturgically as historical events, albeit with a meta-historical significance, cannot simply be theological fictions created by the evangelists as vehicles for imaginative Christology. We should invoke here, with Pope Benedict XV's Biblical Commission, the principle of *lex orandi, lex credendi.*

---

[11]Paragraph 525.

And in any case, such *a priori* determinations are supported by *a posteriori* investigation. Despite allegations to the contrary, the view of some scholars that the infancy Gospels are 'Christian *midrash*', the fanciful telling of tales to bring home the fulfilment of ancient Scriptures in Jesus Christ, is insecurely founded. Authentic midrash looks nothing at all like the Gospels.[12]

In the Roman rite, the feast of the Circumcision of Jesus has been rather obscured in the reform of the Calendar. Though its Gospel is retained the solemnity itself has been transformed into a Marian festival, in honour of the Virgin as, precisely, the God-bearer. Though one understands that Christmas itself, the Theophany, is properly directed to the Child of Bethlehem alone, leaving, then, the octave day for a delayed attention to the Madonna, the *Catechism* is surely right to lay due weight on the significance of Jesus' submission to this painful but essential rite of the Jewish religion. By it, Jesus is inserted into the people of the ancient Covenant; he submits to its Law; and is qualified to share ceremonially in its worship. Although the *Catechism* sees the Lord's circumcision as a type of Christian Baptism (which also initiates into a people, requires the obedience of faith to a revelation, and empowers the candidate to participate in the Liturgy of the Church), this cannot exclude the other great antitype of circumcision, an even more fundamental one, the mystery of the Cross. Just as the ordinary Israelite became a bearer of the Promise through circumcision, and yet was required to become circumcised spiritually by his manner of life, so the Son will suffer in order to effect man's redemption. Jesus' circumcision looks ahead to the bloody sacrifice of Calvary where all Israel's types and shadows are fulfilled.

The Epiphany, the manifestation of the Word made flesh to the Gentiles, in the persons of wise men come from the East,

---

[12]'It was no part of Jewish midrash, or any other Jewish writing-genre in the first century, to invent all kinds of new episodes about recent history in order to advance the claim that the Scriptures had been fulfilled', N. T. Wright, *Who was Jesus?* (London 1992), p. 73. Summarising the conclusions of P. S. Alexander, 'Midrash and the Gospels', in C. M. Tuckett (ed.), *Synoptic Studies* (Sheffield 1984), pp. 1–18, Wright points out that midrash is in fact a tightly controlled commentary on an actual biblical text – something which differs *toto caelo* from what Matthew and Luke attempt in their Gospels.

anticipates the universality of God's salvation as Jesus offers it to all the nations. The *Catechism*, in accordance with its high doctrine of the Jewish inheritance of the Church, treats this mystery in a surprisingly Israel-centred fashion. It draws the conclusion that the pagans cannot recognise Jesus as Lord unless they turn first to the Jews, and enter upon the messianic hope of Israel. But perhaps this interpretation should *not* surprise us, since it corresponds to the liturgical practice of the Church in always reading from the Jewish Scriptures as well as the Christian in her worship. When Augustine sought instruction in the faith from Ambrose he was told to go away and read the book of the prophet Isaiah. The suggestion of some 'advanced' Indian Catholics of the Latin rite that certain Hindu sacred texts might be acknowledged as a *praeparatio evangelica* for the Gospel, and used as an alternative to the Hebrew Bible in the Indian church, met with no favour at Rome. And coming to possess the 'dignity of Israel' is how both St Leo the Great and the Roman Liturgy of the present time treat the journey of the magi. Once again, however, this should not be taken to exclude other, equally traditional, forms of exegesis of this event which are rich in catechetical possibilities. In his kindness, God even allowed astrology, foolish as it is, to succeed this once for those who, in purity of heart, set out on this strange expedition. They brought before the Face of the invisible God now made visible the gold of their love for the deity, the incense of their reverence, the myrrh of their suffering – gifts later to be reinterpreted christologically as gold for Christ's kingship, frankincense for his divinity, and myrrh for his redeeming Passion.

If the Circumcision has shifted from being a christological to a Mariological feast in modern Western Catholicism, the Purification has moved in the reverse direction, becoming, as in the *Catechism*, a commemoration of the Christ who was presented in the Temple. In the Lord's encounter with Symeon and Anna, an echo of the Byzantine name for the Presentation, Christ is recognised by these obscure holy people – one of each gender, conveniently for sexual even-handedness! – as the long-awaited Messiah of Israel, as well as the light of the Gentiles and – a darker designation, 'sign of contradiction'.

Jesus, in order to be the 'First-born from the dead', and so be recognised as the 'First-born of all creation', must first make the offering not, as had his mother and father on this occasion, of 'a pair of turtle doves or two young pigeons' (Luke 2:24) but of his body on the Cross. A sword will pass through his mother's soul at the costly redemption made on Calvary's tree: a vital theme in Catholic devotion to 'our Lady of Sorrows'. The Flight into Egypt and the Massacre of the Innocents caused by the opposition of the Herodian monarchy to messianic rumour, continue this theme, prefiguring the full realisation of the evangelist John's judgment on the Messiah's fate, 'He came to his own, but his own did not receive him' (John 1:11).

The mysteries of the hidden life of Jesus consist on the one hand of his sharing in the realities of family and work – which have made up, for the vast majority of human beings on this planet, the chief concerns of everyday life, and on the other hand, of the one singular event which punctuates the unbroken line of this extraordinary ordinariness – the episode of the Finding in the Temple. As well as recording words of Pope Paul VI at Nazareth, which have found their way into the Roman Liturgy of the Hours, and which laud the holy house as a 'school of the Gospel' in matters not only of family and work but also *silence*, the *Catechism* presents the submission of Jesus to his parents as both a reflection of his obedience to the eternal Father and a prefiguration of the conforming of his human will to the divine will on Holy Thursday, in the Garden of Gethsemane. The obedience of the divine Son-made-man to his mother and adoptive father, and to the ordinary familial and communitarian norms they represented, constitutes both a beginning of his work of re-establishing what Adam's disobedience destroyed and the Gospel foundation of the Church's own concern for the structures of the family and of society, seen as pre-given in the 'natural law'. Nothing, however, can make the family of Nazareth into a typical human family – which is why it is an archetype of the Catholic home, not an instance of it. And yet the holy family was not sacred because it knew no troubles (as the Losing in the Temple shows!). It was sacred because of the resources of grace it brought to those negative moments, and the way human freedom struggled with and triumphed over those negativities, until by continuing conversion and sacrifice it became in Mary the nucleus of the Church of the Resurrection.

The hidden life of Jesus at Nazareth is also a life of labour, and Catholicism has seen in this a consecration of work: a divine declaration that the penal aspects of toil are not the whole story. At the same time, the Church marvels at the contrast between the infinite work of the God–man in his divine nature and the finite work in which he consented, in his humanity, to find meaning and fulfilment. All that is implicit in the *Catechism's* citation of a pope's words in that town of Galilee (Paragraph 533).

It treats the Losing and Finding in the Temple as the glimpsing of Jesus' sense of consecration to his mission, itself the consequence in his human sensibility of the eternal Sonship which is his outside of time. A fuller account would see the episode as an anticipation of Jesus' coming of age, in the following year, when he would be held bound by all the commandments, not only ethical but also ceremonial, of the Torah. In the week after Passover, when doctors of the Law would give semi-popular lectures on the Temple terrace to mark the festal season, Jesus marks his own approaching entry in fullness into the covenant by asserting the primacy of his Father, *vis-à-vis* his human parents.

In this sense the Tarrying in the Temple forms a fitting prelude to the mysteries of the public life which open with Jesus' Baptism. The *Catechism* presents Jesus' Baptism as a major Christophany or disclosure of who he is. Like a second Epiphany, it manifests him as Israel's Messiah and Son of God. It speaks of the Baptism as Jesus' 'acceptance and inauguration' of his mission as the Suffering Servant.[13] Here the text prescinds from speaking outright of Jesus' coming to consciousness of his saving mission – but it does not exclude our treating the Baptism as a moment of breakthrough *par excellence* in a developing awareness. Since the New Testament itself alludes to the growth of the child not only in stature but also in wisdom, we are licensed in speaking of the Incarnation as 'augmentative':

---

[13] Paragraph 536.

the Word seizes and appropriates those fresh aspects to the individual humanity of Jesus which are generated by his burgeoning development. The *Catechism*, however, remains, justifiably, more interested in the objective than the subjective significance of the event: theological ontology rather than psychology, what it means rather than how it felt. And there is indeed a 'splendour of doctrine' shining out from the Baptism, that descending into the depths which Byzantine artists often portrayed as an analogue of the Crucifixion, where the Lord went down beneath the waters of death and Sheol. To 'fulfil all righteousness' (Matthew 3:15) that is, to submit himself totally to the will of the Father, the Lord Jesus undergoes this anticipation of the 'baptism' of his sacrificial death. The *Catechism* makes four main points in its exposition of the implications of this event for our salvation. First, Jesus' self-identification with sinners is accepted by the Father whose 'voice' expresses delight in the Son's action. Secondly, the Holy Ghost, possessed by Jesus from the first moment of his conception, now begins to 'rest' on him – that is, to constitute him as the source of the Spirit's active presence for all humanity whose mediator with the Father this beloved Servant is. Thirdly, in the language of apocalyptic, the heavens, closed by Adam's sin, are thrown open again: the ready intercourse of God and the world is resumed. Fourthly, this is not simply restoration but a new beginning: the waters of the Jordan, sanctified by the descent of the Son and the Spirit, are the prelude of a new creation, for the world of spirit and matter, unified as these are in man, the microcosm of creation, will be re-made by the death and Resurrection of the Son. And, looking ahead to the subject it must treat once its exploration of the Creed is over, the *Catechism* points out that, by his or her own Baptism of water and the Holy Spirit, the individual Christian becomes identified sacramentally with Jesus who, in his (archetypal) Baptism gave us a sign of his eventual Pass-over to a new life. Without a share in the humility and vicarious repentance of the Son, the wholly Innocent One, we, who are far from innocent, cannot be re-born as 'sons in the Son'.

The experience of the Baptism, as the *Catechism* now reminds its readers, had led Jesus to embrace a period of solitude in the

Judaean desert. There he had felt Satan entice him to try out the various possibilities implicit in the power of the divine Sonship thus confirmed. The Gospels present him as the new Adam who, unlike the first, stayed faithful; the perfect Israel of God fully obedient to the divine call. Seeking the Father's will through prayer and fasting, he dismissed the Devil's promptings as presumption and evil temptation.

Christ's work of 'recapitulating' – summing up, and thus fulfilling – all human existence in God involves a negative recapitulation of the Fall of Adam. As St Irenaeus presents Christ's work of deliverance (curiously, the *Catechism*, devoted to the Lyonnese doctor, does not cite him here): a movement backwards, taking over again what man has done awry, is also a movement forwards – the bringing into existence of something new, a man of earthly flesh and blood who is simultaneously the image of God and like God. In the Temptations, Christ takes his stand against Lucifer, forcing his way through the Fall and emerging on the other side in God's sinless creation. But the place of his final emerging will be his Resurrection on the third day. As the *Catechism* puts it, Jesus' victory in the wilderness signalises in advance the victory of the Cross.

Contrary to a certain theopaschite tendency which has entered some modern Catholic theology from Lutheranism, the *Catechism* does not feel obliged to maintain that Jesus was altogether in the same boat as we are. Despite its superficial rhetorical appeal, a God–man who is in rather a mess is not a Saviour. In Jesus' case, temptation could come only from without, never from within; nor was the result at all uncertain. However, this did not make his struggle less intense. To suffer temptation but without the possibility of sinning was for one whose sinlessness made his spiritual fibre as man more perfect and delicate than ours a keener sort of moral suffering than any we have known. The *Catechism* does not dilate on these matters of the interior psychology of the Lord, but, consonant with its stress on the 'revelatory, redemptive and recapitulatory' character of his mysteries, emphasises that his temptations were *for us*. At once a disclosure of his solidarity with sinners (as the Letter to the Hebrews will argue) and a triumph of spiritual warfare in our nature, the Temptations in the Wilderness constitute an invitation to Christians to fight on against evil within and without, which is why the Church each Lent asks her members to go out with Jesus into the desert.

The *Catechism's* account of the public ministry is dominated – and here all contemporary New Testament scholarship will applaud – by the concept of the 'Kingdom'. The preaching of the Kingdom – the imminent reign, ushered in thanks to his own presence and activity, of the loving mercy of the Father – extends from the moment when Jesus hears of the imprisonment of his Precursor (by Herod Antipas, at the Machaerus fortress, down on the Dead Sea) to the messianic entry into Jerusalem, celebrated by the Church of all rites on Palm Sunday. Jesus' message was one of the unconditional nearness of the Father's love and mercy which will become the sovereign norm of the world ('the Kingdom') for those who accept it by repentant faith. His message is embodied in his own practice – his warmth towards those who, though morally guilty, accept the grace of forgiveness and begin to live out the feast of the Kingdom. It is also demonstrated in his judgment on those who are hardened in self-righteousness.

This message is sealed by acts of power – what the *Catechism* calls 'signs of the Kingdom of God', in which the divine Son reverses the disintegrating effects of the activity of the evil angels by his exorcisms, restoring men and women to the sanity which is their birthright, since they were created in the Logos, the archetype of rationality. It is sealed too by miracles of healing and recreation in which power goes out from the Son to make good the deficiencies of the nature created through him, as well as to furnish signs of the yet more wonderful re-creating of human nature – its raising up to share in the Father's grace and glory.

Either straightforwardly or subtly, with vigorous brush-strokes or delicate insinuation, the *Catechism* simultaneously describes the public ministry for its own sake and as a prefigurement of some principal features in the life of the Church. The fellowship Jesus enjoyed with his disciples is, after all, the first sketch of the apostolic community, the gathering of a structured people, a hierarchical society, around his saving person. The assembly of the disciples, as they listen to the words of Jesus and contemplate his face, is the first instalment of the mystery of the Church, just as the Church is the sacrament of the Kingdom, whose centre is the same Jesus Christ, the Kingdom in person as Origen in the East and Cyprian in the West call him, for his kingly office it is to unify human beings and let them be a corporate self-offering to the Father.

If the coming of the Kingdom – in its *foundational* reality (its final consummation must await the Parousia) – only happens with Christ's death and Resurrection, since these bring down the barriers of guilt and finitude which separate men from the Father, we can nonetheless observe Jesus in the course of his ministry gradually preparing for the Church, which will be the Kingdom's first adumbration.

The *Catechism* treats the life of the disciples with their Master as a blueprint for that of the Church in eight main ways. First, as already indicated, the Church will be a Christ-centred assembly. What the *Catechism* has already said of divine revelation – that its centre is Jesus Christ – it can hardly deny of the Church, which is the bearer of that revelation and the realisation of its practical imperatives. Secondly, the Church will be catholic: it will be a home for all peoples, though a faithful remnant of Israel will remain its original, and ever-honoured membership. Onto this olive-tree the wild sprigs of the Gentile cultures will be grafted. Thirdly, entrance to the Church will come about through receiving the Word of Christ by a faithful assent. There can be no purely cultural Catholicism; all authentic Catholicism is evangelical, entailing the lively reception of the Gospel message. Fourthly, the privileged members of the Church will not be the rich and powerful but the 'poor and the little ones'. As the seventeenth century French bishop Jacques-Bénigne Bossuet declared in his sermon 'On the Eminent Dignity of the Poor in the Church':

> In the world, the rich have all the advantages and hold the first rank, whereas in the Kingdom of Jesus Christ, pre-eminence belongs to the poor, who are the first-born of the Church and its true children. [Again,] in the world the poor are subject to the rich, and appear to be born only to serve them: on the contrary, in holy Church, the rich are only admitted on the condition that they serve

the poor. [Lastly,] in the world, favours and privileges are for the powerful and rich, the poor sharing in them only by their support: in the Church of Jesus Christ, by contrast, favours and blessings are for the poor. and the rich have no privileges except through their mediation.[14]

There is nothing novel, in other words, about a 'love of preference for the poor' in the community of Jesus. Fifthly, the Church will be a place for the festal reconciliation of sinners. Sixthly, it will perpetuate an interior understanding of the 'mysteries of the kingdom' which the Lord expounded esoterically, for the inner group of the disciples, rather than exoterically, for those still looking for a handle on them, for the crowd. Seventhly, the messianic signs of deliverance, healing and recreation will have an afterlife in the works of mercy, both spiritual and corporeal, performed by the Church. And eighthly and finally, Jesus promises the keys of the kingdom, authority in governance, to the Twelve, and, especially, to Peter. They will be the viziers of the Kingdom, to be succeeded in that dread office by the popes and bishops of the Catholic Church.

The *Catechism's* main example of the anticipation of the Kingdom is not, however, the gradual putting in place of the structures and ethos of the apostolic fellowship but the high point of the mystical experience of the apostles during the historic ministry: the Transfiguration. It was under the lee of Mount Hermon, the northernmost point of a journey of re-education which the Synoptics describe the Master as undertaking towards the close of his ministry, that Jesus had begun to teach the disciples his understanding of Messiahship, entailing as this did identification with a Son of Man who could only be glorious if he was first humiliated and killed (Mark 8:31–32a and parallels). Their amazed and negative reaction, vocalised by Peter, was followed by the experience of the Transfiguration of Christ on the mountain's summit. Through this lifting of the veil of time and space, they were able to see their Master in the company of the greatest figures of Israel's

---

[14]'Sermon pour le dimanche de la Septuagésime', in *Oeuvres choisies de Bossuet*, vi (Versailles 1822), p. 16.

history, Moses and Elijah, and also to glimpse something of his deeper mystery. As the *Catechism* presents matters, by showing them his refulgent glory as the Father's beloved Son, Jesus confirms Peter's confession below the mountain ('You are the Christ, the Son of the living God' (Matthew 16:16), and reveals that to enter into his glory he must go the way of the Cross.

The appearance of Moses and Elijah is highly significant. In the Hebrew Bible they embody the holy warfare of the struggle with evil (personified in Pharaoh in the one case, Jezebel and the gods of Canaan in the other). They are, then, suitable presences for the 'last days' – Jesus' final confrontation with Satan, with sin and with death. When Jesus goes on, after the vision has passed, to predict his forthcoming death, and to caution the disciples not to tell what they have seen until his sufferings are completed, this signifies the intimate connexion between the glory and the Cross which the *Catechism* posits. (Moreover, according to Jewish tradition, Moses and Elijah were taken forward *at their deaths* into the coming glory of the divine reign.) Acclaimed by the Father as his Beloved, to whom the disciples must listen, Jesus uses the opportunity of this mystical disclosure, then, to point his followers to the sacrifice of his dying – a sacrifice that was necessary if his humanity is to become, at the end of all things, the perfect organ of God's self-expression to the world. It coheres with this suggestion that the *Catechism*, following St Thomas, can speak of the Transfiguration as *sacramentum secundae regenerationis*, the 'mystery of our second regeneration' – the final resurrection of the redeemed, which follows, at the end of the ages, our first regeneration in the saving waters of Baptism. The Transfiguration is the sign of humanity on its way to final redemption in God, the dawn of a history of joy in the midst of the unanswered suffering of the world. The wonderful text from Augustine's Sermons which closes the *Catechism's* account:

> The Way came down to be exhausted on his journey; the Spring goes down to suffer thirst; and you refuse to suffer?

makes this mystery, and its liturgical celebration, a great stimulus to courage and hope.

From the Transfiguration the *Catechism* passes directly to the last major event in Jesus' life before the Passion: the final journey of his life to Jerusalem. As is well-known, the Synoptics record only one such visit, but this is probably in the wake of St Matthew's deliberately schematic account of Jesus' preaching – from Galilee, through Judaea, to Jerusalem. Matthew himself is well aware that Jesus' journey to Jerusalem for his Passion was by no means his only acquaintance with the capital (cf. 23:37b). Every pious Jew would want to go up when they could for the pilgrimage feasts. The *Catechism* gives us a flurry of texts indicative of Jesus' attitude at this turning-point, whose burning question must be, in the authors' own words, 'How will Jerusalem welcome her Messiah?' Taking the holy city as the type of the Church, which is also known as Zion, or Zion's Daughter, the *Catechism* recalls how the Lion of Judah, David's Son, entered 'his' city on the foal of an ass – thus turning upside down all the symbolism of legitimate kingship. Christ the King will win the Church his bride not by cleverness nor a display of strength but by 'the humility that bears witness to the Truth'[15] – as his confession before Pilate, who would ask, half-seriously, if he *were* a king, attests (John 18:37).

The *Catechism* devotes its remaining hundred or so christological paragraphs to the Paschal mystery of Jesus' saving death and Resurrection, with a coda on his Parousia. Here above all it attempts to hold together the Church's Jesus with the historian's Jesus, since the theological claim of the risen Christ on the road to Emmaus that it 'was needful for the Christ to suffer these things and enter thus his glory' (Luke 24:26–27; 44–45) can be elucidated by historical investigation of the circumstances in which Jesus died, with a view to gaining an improved understanding of 'the meaning of the Redemption'.[16]

A phenomenon closely related to the Passion and one which any 'life of Jesus', however rudimentary, must explain is the way Jesus managed to raise up against him an alliance of the most disparate forces in the Jewish society of his day. Anyone who could simultaneously alienate Sadducces and Herodians,

---

[15]Paragraph 559.
[16]Paragraph 573.

Pharisees and the pagan Roman power, must certainly have been an unusual figure. The *Catechism* notes, however, that despite the fact that some of the strongest uses of negative language found on the lips of Jesus in the Gospels are directed against Pharisaic Jews, there are also unmistakable signs in their pages of good relations with individual Pharisees, a number of whose spiritual positions were, in terms of Jesus' own message, 'not far from the Kingdom' (Mark 12:34). Nonetheless, Jesus found himself the victim of charges of blasphemy and false prophecy, accusations which, if sustained in litigation under Israel's sacred law would have led to his execution by stoning. That he was to become rather a *crucified* Messiah is entirely the consequence of Roman imperial intervention.

The *Catechism* explains the hostility of a weird and wonderful variety of contemporary Jews by the coincidence of three senses in which Jesus might be regarded as undermining the central religious institutions – including there cognitive institutions, *beliefs* – of the chosen people.

It chooses to mention first the fact that Jesus' teaching and example relativised the importance of obedience to the Law considered as a self-sufficient totality – whether that be thought of in written terms (as with the Sadduccees) or in terms both written and oral (as with the Pharisees). What the Lord did was to propose an interpretation of the Law which fulfilled its precepts by transcending them. On the questions of, notably, the laws governing the use of clean and unclean foods, and the observance of the Sabbath, Jesus showed a sovereign freedom in his handling of the inherited patrimony of Jewish practice and reflection. As the *Catechism* puts it, he treated these aspects of the ceremonial or ritual Torah as 'pedagogical':[17] as symbolic vehicles for truths of wider application about human integrity and perfection in the first case, and man's relation to God's work of creation in the second. Although at times Jesus argued like a rabbi, he did not offer his interpretations as theses for consideration by doctors in the schools. Innovatory and sweeping though they might be, they were laid down as definitive

---

[17] Paragraph 582.

determinations of the divine purpose in granting the Torah to Israel.

Secondly, Jesus' teaching, despite his devout attendance at the Temple liturgy, tended ultimately to peripheralise the sanctuary of Zion, previously the central locus of the sacred for the Jewish religion, at any rate since the Deuteronomic reform of the seventh century before the Christian era. Pointing out that the Cleansing of the Temple implies not hostility but zeal for his Father's house, and accepting the claim of the Johannine tradition that much of Jesus' teaching was given in its precincts, the *Catechism* makes the unusual suggestion that Jesus identified himself so completely with the Temple as the 'site' of communion with God as to infer from his own imminent Passion the Temple's equally imminent destruction. It may be in order to add an ecclesiological reference, for the Messiah is never without his community.... . In his response to Peter's confession at Caesarea Philippi, Jesus defines his aim as the messianic task of building a living 'temple', as on rock, secure against decay, the temple of the Last Days. Jesus was referring to the *eschatological* temple, which in Hebrew prophecy symbolised the final meeting-place of God and man, the locus of their definitive communion. As the final revealer of God's will and the agent through whom that will was to be realised, constructing this temple fell to him personally, though he could not achieve it until first he had become victorious over the anti-God powers at work in the world – sin and death – and thus become enthroned at God's right hand.

This stupendous claim brings us to the third of the Jewish *gravamina* against Jesus, in the *Catechism's* reckoning. Jesus' convictions about his own identity – expressed tacitly or explicitly, discreetly to the disciples or more publicly – called into question the very character of Jewish monotheism if this be considered as, in the *Catechism's* words, 'faith in the one God whose glory no man can share'.[18] Even were we to lay aside, as permitting too insecure access to the *ipsissima verba Jesu*, the testimony of the Fourth Gospel, we would still be left with the

[18] Paragraph 576.

report of the Synoptic tradition that Jesus identified his own attitudes to others, in a context of salvation, with God's own attitude to them. In fact, the *Catechism* might have made more in this regard of the titles of Jesus in the Synoptic tradition and notably of the accumulation of meaning which comes from the aggregating of 'Messiah', 'Son', and 'Son of Man'. For, as no mere messianic pretender, but one who claimed to be the ever-living messianic Son of God, participating in the divine prerogatives *vis-à-vis* the world, only two judgments on this point were possible. Either Jesus' claim was blasphemous effrontery, or the common Jewish doctrine would have to undergo a profound transformation from within. And in any case the *Catechism* treats St John's Gospel as furnishing us with, at the least, the *ipsissima vox Jesu* – the semantic thrust of Jesus' historical utterance, even if with some modification of the lexical terms in which he spoke. And this is plausible if we regard the Johannine tradition as specialising in historical material come down by two routes not explored in the Synoptics: the debates of Jesus with scribal experts, notably in the context of the liturgical life of the Temple, on the one hand, and, on the other, that most intimate part of the esoteric teaching of Jesus to his disciples which is constituted by the giving of his last will and testament, in the 'Farewell Discourse' of the fourteenth to the seventeenth chapters of St John. For it is in the first setting that we can hear him say 'I and the Father are one' (John 10:30), and in the second overhear the claim that 'his person makes present and reveals the Name of God' – as the *Catechism* paraphrases two verses of that speech (John 17:6 and 26).

The *Catechism* sets its theology of the atoning death of Christ within a more circumstantial account of his trial – for this death was, empirically speaking, a judicial execution, though even here the authors' main aim is to comment on the vexed question of Jewish 'deicide', something which requires, evidently, a properly theological adjudication.

While recognising the complexity of the trial accounts in the Gospels (Jesus' position as a defendant was at the interface of the Jewish and Roman jurisdictions), the *Catechism* is chiefly concerned not to reconstruct the legal process involved but –

by way of appeal to wider considerations – to exonerate the Jews (whether the Jerusalem crowd, the religious authorities of Judaism, Jews of the time of Jesus as a whole or the Jewish people considered as a moral unity throughout subsequent history) from responsibility for the death of the Messiah.[19] It would of course be excessive to say that all Jews were opposed to Jesus' claims and mission. Quite apart from the *chaburah*, or inner group of disciples, and the holy women who lingered at the Cross when the majority of the former fled, the *Catechism* specifically singles out, on the evidence of the Book of the Acts of the Apostles, numerous members of the priestly caste of Judaism as well as a more modest number of Pharisees as among the first converts to the new faith. The dreadful cry of the crowd, 'His blood be on us and on our children!' (Matthew 27:25), like the ruthless determination of the high priest that one man's death (however unmerited) is preferable to the perishing of the whole people (John 11:49–50), are charitably assigned to ignorance – following the example of one of Jesus' own last words from the Cross (Luke 23:34), and Peter's sermon in the Portico of Solomon (Acts 3:17). The *Catechism* recognises, however, that a number of the apostolic speeches in Acts do contain 'collective reprovals' of Jewish hearers, and does not seek to whitewash totally those involved, leaving judgment to God alone.[20] Both historically and in terms of the logic of salvation history as set forth in, for instance, Jesus' parable of The Landlord and his Tenants (Matthew 21:33–46), it may be more realistic to allow a degree of guilt not only to the chief actors but also, by way of collusion, to a supporting cast, but, with that testimony to Western piety which is the 'Act of Consecration to the Sacred Heart', add:

> Of old they called down on themselves the blood of the Saviour. May it now descend on them – a laver of redemption and love.

Reference to forms of piety may remind the reader that the

---

[19] See J. McDade S.J., 'The Jewish People in the New Catechism', *The Month* CCLV, 1518 (1994), pp. 237–239.
[20] Paragraph 597.

'act of contrition' most commonly used by penitents in the Latin Church gives as a motive for repentance that my sins have 'crucified my loving Saviour Jesus Christ'. The *Catechism's* chief dogmatic point in regard to the Lord's judicial murder is that 'sinners were the authors ... of all the sufferings that the divine Redeemer endured'.[21] In a reprise of its predecessor, the *Roman Catechism* commissioned by Trent, the new book treats witting Christian trespasses far more severely than the unwitting misdeeds of the Jews who failed to recognise the Lord of Glory.

How, then, does the *Catechism* expound the significance of the death of Jesus, which has become, transmuted into the visual image of the Crucifix, the emblem of the Christian religion? Essentially it interprets the redeeming death of the Lord by a soteriology of *sacrifice*. There are various 'theories', 'models', 'motifs' of the Atonement: which of these terms we shall use depends on the degree to which a central image ('motif'), has developed an organising power which affects a wide range of Christian discourse ('model'), and eventually, it may be, come to found a systematic analysis of its subject-matter ('theory'). In electing to award the palm to the image of the all-inclusive Sacrifice, the makers of the *Catechism* have not necessarily committed themselves to a repudiation of its rivals. They will, however, be insisting that other themes in the rich panoply of imaginative forms used by the New Testament writers to bring out the significance of the Lord's death and Resurrection must be approached along this avenue.

But first we must register some preliminaries. The *Catechism* clears the decks for its theology of the Atonement in two moves. First, any account of the death of Jesus which sees it as the crown of the redemptive activity of God towards the world (however that be understood) must necessarily reject the view that the death in question has the status of mere facticity. It cannot simply be by the play of circumstance that Jesus died, and died in the way he did. Rather was it in his wise foreknowledge that God willed the nexus of secondary causalities whose operation nailed the Christ to the Tree,

---

[21] Paragraph 598.

permitting as he did so (not directly intending, therefore) those actions which, within that wider totality, were at any rate objectively sinful if not subjectively guilty. Secondly, this death, predestined by God, was *for us*. It was meant to bring good, and more specifically religious good, that is, a good which has its identity in the context of the world's relation to God and must be counted therefore an overarching good, for God is the supreme end of man. This the *Catechism* expresses by calling the divine plan of salvation, whose central axis is the putting to death of God's Servant, the Just One, 'a mystery of universal redemption',[22] something it goes on to gloss in terming it also a ransoming which frees human beings from the slavery of sin. That all the New Testament theologies of the Atonement here converge can hardly be doubted, but the *Catechism* selects from the testimonies two soteriological texts, respectively from First Peter (1:18–20) and the Second Letter to the Corinthians (5:21), thus calling to the witness stand the two pillars of the Church of Rome, St Peter and St Paul. More controversially, it claims that Jesus presented the meaning of his own life and redemptive death in terms of the figure of the Suffering Servant of the Oracles of Second Isaiah, and did so not only as the risen Lord, with his transfigured understanding, but as the Man of Sorrows of the historic ministry as well. Although many exegetes, especially among those committed to the Two Document Hypothesis, which finds the earliest expression of at any rate the Synoptic tradition in the Gospel of Mark and an otherwise unknown sayings-source ('Q') derived from comparison of Matthew and Luke, would regard the Suffering Servant theme as a Marcan theologoumenon, it has in fact a secure basis in the wider Gospel tradition thanks to its implicit, but crucial, invocation by Jesus at the institution of the Eucharistic Bread, the Body of the Lord, 'given for you' (cf. I Corinthians 11:24).

Before introducing the actual word 'sacrifice', at the focus of its discussion as this will be, the *Catechism* clarifies the meaning of this 'suffering servanthood' in three regards. If, as

[22]Paragraph 601.

Second Corinthians maintains, God 'made [Christ] sin for our sake', that is, treated him as sin in our favour, this implies no culpability on the part of him who was, in fact, the Sinless One. The *Catechism* explains the cry of apparent abandonment on the Cross ('My God, my God, why hast thou forsaken me?', Mark 15:34) as an expression of profound solidarity with sinners, not a self-numbering among them. On the contrary, it was in the unitive power of the redemptive love which ranged him with his Father that the Son so assumed our persona in our separation from God as to be able to cry out in our name from the depths of our divine estrangement. Here, in Paragraph 603, the *Catechism* offers a masterly statement of the dialectic of union and separation whereby the Son-made-man reappropriated his everlasting relations of communion with the Father precisely by undergoing the experience of Godforsakenness in our sinful flesh. This assertion leads naturally into a second illuminating statement about the Servant's death. It is not an action (or a 'passion', an undergoing) which originates primordially with the Son at all; much less must it be thought of as the contrasting behaviour of the kind and philanthropic Son and the sternly just and headmasterly Father. When we consider the union of wills in the Redeemer, and the singularity of the divine will as between Father and Son we realise how grotesquely distorted such a picture would be. Without invoking here metaphysical divinity, however, the *Catechism* makes the same point by a pastiche of Scripture: precisely in giving over his Son for our sins the Father demonstrated the quality of his own plan, as a work of lovingkindness towards us, heedless of all merit (that is, non-merit!) on our part. Its third point underlines this in one crucial respect: the infinity of the divine generosity is mirrored in the non-limitedness of its human recipients. Christ died that *all* may be saved. This is not of course a prediction (which would mean universalism, one heresy in the theory of grace) but a description of the divine intention (over against another such heresy, Calvinism and its Catholic counterpart, Jansenism).

Christ's communion of love with the Father and, therefore, the coincidence of his human will with the Father's saving design is the immediate context in which the *Catechism* introduces the key term of 'sacrifice'.[23] It speaks of the desire to embrace God's redemptive will as the motive-force of Jesus' whole life; the saving Passion is the rationale of his Incarnation. (It was at any rate, we recall, the first of the four statements of the rationale of the Flesh-taking with which the christological section of the book opened.) It is not asserted that Jesus was always aware in his human mind of the crucial character of his death, but the authors date such consciousness, at least in the mind of his cousin, John, from the moment of the Baptism. Certainly, and *pace* Albert Schweitzer and later critics, who see Jesus' Passion predictions as a result of the failure of his ministry, no current in the stream of Gospel tradition treats Jesus' premonition of his own violent death, and insight into its saving significance, as a tardy development. That is simply exegetical dogmatism, the insistence that all prophecy must be *ex eventu*. That a rejection of radical criticism here does not entail denying the significance of Jesus' personal history in the constitution of his salvational rôle becomes clear when, in the very next paragraph, the *Catechism* speaks of how through his sufferings and death the humanity of the Word '*became* the free and perfect instrument of his divine love which desires the salvation of men'.[24]

Two episodes from the Passion narratives are singled out for special comment before the significance of the Sacrifice on the Hill is finally decanted. The institution of the Eucharist constitutes the solemn interpretation, before the event, of the prophetic gesture of his dying. Declaring the Mass to be, in deliberate inverted commas, the 'memorial' of his Sacrifice, the *Catechism* appeals thereby to the pregnant associations of the biblical term *anamnêsis*, with its connotations of the continuing vitality of a once-for-all event. The later Church has frequently wished to make the identity of Eucharist and Calvary clearer; thus for instance the Anglo-Welsh lay theologian and artist David Jones remarks that

> We speak of the 'Altar of the Cross' only on the *presupposition* that the extra-utile [i.e. symbolic] ritual

[23]Paragraph 606.
[24]Paragraph 609. Italics added.

oblation at the Supper had already placed our Lord in the state of a victim awaiting immolation.[25]

But further thoughts on the relation of identity between the Sacrifice of the Cross and of the Altar must await the time when the *Catechism* deals *ex professo* with the Holy Eucharist. The Agony in the Garden is resolved in the re-appropriated conformity of the Lord's human will with his divine, thus making Jesus the visible embodiment of the Father's saving plan. The suggestion that the prayer 'If it be possible, let this cup pass from me' (Matthew 26:39) reflects the natural shrinking of Jesus' human sensibility, as a *physical* man, from the prospect of imminent death, is already found in the classical discussion of patristic times, that of St Maximus the Confessor.[26] The *Catechism* presents this ontologically founded revulsion of Christ from the Passion in fuller terms. Not only is death unnatural to Jesus as a human being destined, like all men, for eternal life, and one, moreover, who was uniquely a stranger to the sin which is the cause of death. Inasmuch as he is also the Word, consubstantial with the Father, death is supremely alien to him, for he is 'the Author of life' (Acts 3:15) and 'the Living One' (Apocalypse 1:17).

The Cross which Jesus now takes upon his shoulders is a Trinitarian event. The Sacrifice of Christ is the supreme giving of the Father who makes the Son over to men to reconcile them with himself. At the same time, it is the free and loving offering of his life by the Son, in the Holy Spirit, to the Father, for the making good of human disobedience. The Trinity is the eternal form of the Cross; the Cross is the human icon of the Trinity. As Gerald Manley Hopkins wrote in his *Notebooks*:

> This Sacrifice ... is a consequence and shadow of the

---

[25] Cited in R. Hague (ed.), *Dai Greatcoat. A Self-portrait of David Jones in his Letters* (London 1980), p. 231. See further on this my *The Holy Eucharist. From the New Testament to Pope John Paul II* (Dublin 1991), pp. 104–106.

[26] For a full account, see F.-M. Léthel, *Théologie de l'Agonie du Christ. La liberté humaine du Fils de Dieu et son importance théologique mises en lumière par S. Maxime le Confesseur* (Paris 1979). Cf. my *Byzantine Gospel. Maximus the Confessor in Modern Scholarship* (Edinburgh 1993), pp. 100–101.

procession of the Trinity, from which mystery sacrifice takes its rise.[27]

So far, the *Catechism* has spoken of the Son's solidarity with sinful humanity, and the free yet obedient love in which he makes his offering on their behalf. But now, taking its cue from that 'Passion of our Lord Jesus Christ according to Isaiah' which is found in the Songs of the Servant, as well as from Paul's Letter to the Romans, it speaks in the harsher accents which consideration of the unique – and hence lonely – task the Son performed in our nature when, that God's justice might be vindicated and human responsibility upheld, he not only offered but expiated. On Calvary Christ is the substitutionary Victim who repairs, expiates, and makes satisfaction.

Just as the freely willed openness of the person to God through desire and love has an infinite positive dimension which will ultimately be realised in the loving vision of God, so, *because* the human creature is in this way ordered to a communion of life with its Maker there is also, in the self-enclosure which is sin an infinite negative aspect. Sin involves a refusal of an infinite Object – or rather Subject. As this disorder lay in the free will of man, it was at that same level that redressal must take place. As man, the Son of God was capable of making the human gesture of reparation; as the divine Word, the initiative Jesus took had an infinite value.

Moreover, as the *Catechism* now goes on to point out, he could make that offering on behalf of us all, since the Father has made him the new head of all humanity – the Second and Last Adam – by letting the destiny of each and every human being turn on the work of the Son-made-man. Paulinus of Nola brings this truth out well in his poem *Verbum Crucis*:

> Look on thy God, Christ hidden in our flesh.
> A bitter word, the Cross, the bitter sight:
> Hard rind without, to hold the heart of heaven.
> Yet sweet it is; for God upon that tree

---

[27]C. Devlin, S.J. (ed.), *The Sermons and Devotional Writings of Gerard Manley Hopkins* (London 1959), p. 197.

> Did offer up his life: upon that rood
> My Life hung, that my life might stand in God ...

Only Christ, as the God–man, can be the Mediator between God and human beings, yet since he embraces all human beings at the intersection of eternity and time which he inhabits, all can enter into contact with the Paschal mystery, associate themselves with his redeeming Sacrifice. Here, with an explicit mention of the Blessed Virgin Mary, who stood by the Cross, as the paradigmatic Hearer of the Word, the *Catechism* looks ahead to its own later sacramental, ethical and spiritual reflections. The remainder of Paulinus' poem may stand proxy for them here:

> Christ, what am I to give Thee for my life?
> Unless take from Thy hands the cup they hold,
> To cleanse me with the precious draught of death.
> What shall I do? My body to be burned?
> Make myself vile? The debt's not paid out yet.
>
> Whate'er I do, it is but I and Thou,
> And still do I come short, still must Thou pay
> My debts, O Christ, for debts Thyself hadst none.
> What love may balance Thine? My Lord was found
> In fashion like a slave, that so His slave
> Might find himself in fashion like his Lord.
> Think you the bargain's hard, to have exchanged
> The transient for the eternal, to have sold
> Earth to buy Heaven? More dearly God bought me.

The Burial of Christ is not a common topic for theological reflection. Yet both the *Apostolicum*, which the *Catechism* is following, and the Creed of Nicaea–Constantinople take the trouble to note it distinctly from death. The mystery of the Burial belongs with the mystery of the Descent into Hell: the Father willed that the Son should experience death in its fullness, for our sake, and that means in the first instance the natural yet unnatural separation of soul from body of which the body's laying in the sepulchre is the potent sign. But, as the procession of the faithful accompanying the flower-covered bier of Christ on the evening of Good Friday in the Byzantine rite attests, the burial of Christ, insofar as it forms an integral part of our happy salvation, is by no means a matter of unrelieved gloom. Beautifully, the *Catechism* describes it as manifesting the Sabbath rest of God – this time not after his work of creation is completed, but on finishing his work of redemption with its power to bring 'peace to the whole universe'.[28]

The Lord's body, resting in the silence of the grave, remains the body of the eternal Logos. As Gregory of Nyssa's *Catechetical Oration* affirms, the same Person was the meeting-point, the cross-roads, of death and life, supplying a new principle – transcendent inasmuch as he is God, immanent inasmuch as he is man – whereby the mortality of the flesh can pass over into unending life. In this sense, one might add, the Resurrection will complete what the Incarnation started: the divine Son, in taking our frail, contingent, alienated and corrupted nature upon himself – he who is the single Source of all creaturely being as the Word – transferred our origin into him, so as to secure our being from the fate of final dissolution. Baptismal immersion signifies our transfer into him, from the death of sin to newness of life (cf. Romans 6:4).

But the Word also remained the subject of the soul of Christ which, as the Apostles' Creed (but not the Nicene–Constantinopolitan Creed) affirms, descended into Hell, that is, into Sheol, the abode of the dead, the 'Limbo of the Fathers', those who are awaiting the outcome of history. Though the just and the unjust had different experiences of this waiting (something made clear, as the *Catechism* points out, in Jesus' own parable of Dives and Lazarus, Luke 16:22–26), the common feature in their disparate experience is their lack of the vision of God. This is what enables us to locate them in the same theological space.

Eschewing certain speculations of the moderns on the Descent into Hell as the destruction of the state of damnation itself, the *Catechism*, rightly, keeps close to the biblical witness in treating the Descent, with First Peter, as the proclamation of

[28] Paragraph 624.

the Good News of salvation to those who would be redeemed by Christ (cf. I Peter 4:6). The Descent is at one and the same time the lowest pitch of the suffering of the Passion and the beginning of the Resurrection. For, on the one hand, death is the absolute opposite of the God who is God not of the dead but of the living, and yet, on the other, Christ's soul, in glory on its separation from the body, actively communicated its condition of beatitude to the waiting souls of the just – as in the great Byzantine Easter icons where Christ takes Adam by the hand. And citing the moving anonymous homily for Holy Saturday, now used in the Roman Office of Readings for that day, the *Catechism* speaks of the silence of this day as filled with action: the Descent into Hell redeems the past, for the redemptively causal power of the Lord's glorified humanity can work not only forwards but backwards also.

To speak of Christ's glorified *humanity*, however, is to suppose the transfiguration of not just his soul but his body likewise, and this brings us to the *Catechism's* treatment of the Resurrection. To call it an event at once historical and transcendent would sum up its approach.[29] In exultant tones it proclaims the Resurrection to be the culminating truth of faith in Christ. It rubs the point in by summoning all the recognised criteria of theological epistemology to its side. The Resurrection of the Lord was believed and experienced as the central plank of their belief system by the apostolic community; Tradition transmitted it as foundational; it is an established datum of the New Testament documents; along with the Cross of Christ, it was essential to the preaching of the Paschal mystery. Noteworthy is the final reference there to the Cross: for a Western Catholicism, accused of 'staurocentricity', that is, an inappropriately unilateral emphasis on the death of Christ, has no desire to swing over into an equally unwarranted exclusivism of concern with the Resurrection, just as an Eastern Catholicism, which shares with its separated Eastern Orthodox counterpart a vivid sense of Paschal joy should never forget the price at which the Easter victory was bought.

The Catechism will have it that the Resurrection was not an

---

[29] Paragraph 639.

event so totally meta-historical in character that it left no immediate trace in history. In one sense the Resurrection of Jesus falls within the ambit of the historian and may be studied by his methods. It had manifestations of a kind that can be historically registered: notably the Resurrection appearances, as for instance catalogued by Paul writing to Corinth as early as the year 56, and the empty tomb. The latter, while not coercive proof of anything (it might have multiple explanation), remains an 'essential sign'.[30] What it is a sign of, at the historical level, is shown in the appearances of the Risen One. The *Catechism* in countering the sceptical rejoinder that it must have been Easter faith which created the experience of the resurrected Jesus, rather than the other way round, deals with an objection at least as old as Goethe. For the German poet, 'They are celebrating the Resurrection of the Lord, for they themselves are resurrected'. But what 'they' – the disciples – in fact experienced was fear and doubt, and what awakened joy and jubilation was something other than themselves. They were the ones marked out by death, but the Crucified and Buried One was alive. The *Catechism* insists on the true corporality of the Risen Lord, while also presenting his risen body as now wholly the instrument of his divine-human personality, subject not to the normal constraints of space and time but only to the dominion of the Father. But to grasp the significance of the glorified body of the Lord, and hence the ultimate meaning of the empty tomb, the *Catechism* is obliged to shift gear. To see the Resurrection as an event in history is not enough; it must also be regarded as a transcendent event, one which does not belong, simply, with the series of events that make up the present world-order but establishes the conditions of a new order, a new creation. Here the organs of perception are not those of physiology, but those of faith, the supernaturally-equipped minds and hearts of the apostolic fellowship.

Through the mighty working of the Spirit the Father has so raised up the mortal humanity of the Son that our nature now lives for ever in glory: that is, within the relations of communion

---

[30]Paragraph 640.

of the Trinitarian Persons. The divine Word, having once stepped forth into visibility in his Incarnation, does not – as Balthasar remarks in his profound theology of the Paschal Mystery – return once again to the invisible.[31] The Son-made-man is now brought out, moreover, from under the control of human destructiveness, as of death itself, into a re-created world where the Father at last fulfils the promise inscribed in man's being at the original creation, but constantly spoiled by man himself. Humanity is thrown open to the intimate, irreversible, redemptive and transfiguring action of God. Here we see how right the *Catechism* is to stress the unity of the Resurrection in both its historical and transcendent senses: the historian's Easter and the Church's. Unless there were some element of physical continuity between Jesus and the risen Lord – if it were not the earthly, and hence bodily, life of the rabbi from Nazareth that was this unheard of transformation's subject – then the proclamation of a new creation would be without purchase on the material cosmos.

The salvational bearings of the Resurrection, as the *Catechism* charts them, are far-reaching. The Easter triumph means the vindication of Jesus: divine ratification of all he did and taught. It is the realisation not of his promises alone but of the entire promise-fulfilment structure of the Hebrew Bible – and hence of Israel's waiting on God in all ages. For Jesus himself, it is the confirmation of his claim to be personally identical with the Lord of life; for his followers, which means potentially all humanity, it is entry on newness of life through justification, the receipt, through the acceptance of Christ's atoning Sacrifice by the Father, of God's forgiveness. It is also the turning of forgiven friends into brothers, and so adoptive sonship of the Father for the children of men. Finally, the Resurrection is the source and principle of the future raising up of our own bodies. As St Bonaventure declared in his Sermon for Passion Sunday:

> It would be unbecoming for the Head to be beautiful and immortal while the members were corruptible and ugly.

---

[31]H. U. von Balthasar, *Mysterium Paschale: the Mystery of Easter* (E.t. Edinburgh 1990), pp. 206–207.

The separation of soul from body mars the beauty of human nature as God made it. The divine Bridegroom's aim in assuming human nature, and dying and rising in it, is to draw his Bride, redeemed mankind, into his own beauty – first in the soul, by grace, then in the body, by glory.

And so the *Catechism* draws its exposition of the christological portion of the Creed to an end by considering the mysteries of hope: the Ascension, the Session at the Right Hand, and the Return in Glory.

The simplest way to think of the Ascension is as the last of the Resurrection appearances (with the exception of the, confessedly out-of-time, 'shewing' to St Paul on the Damascus Road). But the *Catechism*, along with Tradition at large, does not wish to leave matters there. Jesus' reluctance that Mary Magdalene should touch him before he has ascended to the Father (John 20:17) signals a 'difference of manifestation'[32] between the glory of the risen Christ and that of the ascended Lord. The Ascension of Christ is an ascent in order to fill all things with himself, so that what follows on the Ascension is not absence but a new mode of presence. He left us in the mode of our presence to each other so as to return to us in the mode of God's presence to man. In particular, the *Catechism* sees the Ascension, with the spectacles of the Writer to the Hebrews, as the initiation of Jesus' heavenly intercession for humanity as our High Priest. It is the beginning of the Christian Liturgy, the mystery of worship in which we have access to the Father, and of which the ascended Christ is both the central figure and the principal actor.

The prayer of our great High Priest, being that of one who is in both divine and human natures, and who lives in the latter in its glorified condition, totally transparent to the former, must necessarily be efficacious for the world. The Ascension cannot be separated, therefore, from the Session at the Right Hand of the Father. The praying of the ascended Christ can mean nothing less than the inauguration of that Kingdom foretold by the prophets and won in blood and tears by the

---

[32] Paragraph 660.

meritorious Passion of the messianic Son.

Finally, he will come again in glory to judge both the quick and the dead. The *Catechism* strikes a balance, in its exposition of this clause, between realised and future eschatology. Christ is not only the once and future king; he *already* reigns through his Church in history. This is the true triumphalism of the Crucified Messiah: *Christus vincit, Christus regnat, Christus imperat.* Since Christ has conquered (sin and death), he naturally reigns, and does so imperially. But this imperial office of the Lord Jesus is not yet exercised in the 'power and great glory' which his apocalyptic discourse to the disciples on the eve of the Passion foretold (Luke 21:27). As we look at the world around us (and at the world found present in the Church who, as the Bride of Christ, all glorious within, is by no means as yet all glorious without), we soon see that it falls far short of the Kingdom described for us in the Roman Liturgy on the feast of Christ the King:

> a Kingdom of truth and life,
> a Kingdom of holiness and grace,
> a Kingdom of justice, love and peace.

Nonetheless, we are in the last phase of salvation history, whose last hour has already struck. The *Catechism*, echoing the Letter to the Romans, finds that only the absence of a persuasive preaching to Israel, and to all the nations of the earth (at any rate, one can suppose, representatively) stands between us and the Parousia of the Lord – though it admits that the prayer of Christians ('Come, Lord Jesus!', Apocalypse 22:20) would also help.

Not that the *Catechism* expects for the future road of the Church a tale simply of sweetness and light. Rather does it commit itself to an expectation of a 'Passion of the Church', in which, by way of preliminary to the Lord's coming, the Church-body will know, in a fashion hitherto unparalleled, the messianic birth-pangs so far experienced only by its blessed Head. Somewhat in the style of the Edwardian priest-novelist Robert Hugh Benson's *Lord of the World* it takes the Anti-Christ spoken of by Scripture to be a pseudo-Messiah who manages to raise humanity to the status of a (false) god. Rehearsals for his coming take the form of millenarianism in its numerous forms – whether religious (as with a charismatic chiliasm, expecting the 'thousand year reign' of saints on earth) or political (and here both Utopian and social-scientific versions are possible, as witness the wilder excesses of 'liberation theology'). And if that evaluation seems severe, the ground for its making is worth pondering: for what all such movements have in common is the will to press history to a final conclusion through bypassing, or ignoring, the Last and Universal Judgment. The world which will supervene on that final determination of all things will be at once more wonderful than ours and more terrible. Scripture speaks of it both as a banquet where all the nations will feast together in the presence of the Most High, and as a day of lamentation when the tribes of the earth will wail for him who they have pierced. Its common factor, therefore, is that it will be a world of the most lucid moral and spiritual clarity where the mercy and justice of God are revealed in the opened heart of Christ, and the thoughts of *all* hearts are laid bare.

VI

*Professing the Faith: The Creed on the Holy Spirit**

The *Catechism* opens its section on the Spirit of God – and the multifarious aspects of the saving economy he animates – by linking pneumatology, the doctrine of the Spirit, to Christology, the doctrine of the Son which we have just surveyed. Appealing to the Pauline Letters: no one can confess Jesus as the eternal Son without the Holy Spirit (I Corinthians 12:3), while it is through the Spirit that the Son enables Christians to share his posture, crying 'Abba, Father!' (Galatians 4:6). This is not simply a matter of effecting a smooth transit from the middle to the concluding segments of the Creed – or the penultimate to the ultimate chapters of this book! Reference to the Holy Spirit proved unavoidable in expounding the opening, foundational statements of the *Catechism* on the subject of Jesus Christ, so here likewise the Spirit is immediately identified as the One who places the believer in contact with the mystery of the Son. There can be no better place than a catechism, itself intended in the last resort for the instruction of neophytes, at which to recall this truth. For

> the Holy Spirit in the Church communicates to us, intimately and personally, the life that originates in the Father and is offered to us in the Son.[1]

---

* = *Catechism*, Paragraphs 683–1065.
[1] Paragraph 683.

And a text from Irenaeus' *Demonstration of the Apostolic Preaching* reminds us that, though the Spirit may be last among the Trinitarian Persons to our consciousness – as he was certainly last to have his Godhead solemnly recognised by the teaching office of the Church, nonetheless he is first in the order of the divine gracious activity whereby we come to know the Father through the Son, thanks to the communion established by Baptism, with its grace of spiritual re-birth. It is the Spirit who brings men to the Son, that the Son may present them to the Father. He who is unconditionally first in the order of our subjective transformation, is but the last in the objective revelation of the Holy Trinity. Here we are thinking not of the 'spirit' of God, inchoately conceived as the power of the divine creative and redemptive causality, but of the personal Spirit of the Father and the Son – a Possessing of the divine Essence distinct from either of theirs. The indwelling Holy Spirit of Christ whose secret presence and action makes possible all theological faith in Jesus, and all practical obedience to him in the mission of the Church, remains himself easily overlooked. Profoundly, the Russian Orthodox dogmatician Vladimir Lossky found in this striking fact, with which the *Catechism's* pneumatology opens, the key to the personal identity – the unique *hypostasis* – of the Spirit. As the go-between God, at once the ever-living substantial relationship between the Father and the Son, and the personal form of their relation with the human creation, the Holy Spirit most characteristically delights in anonymity. Only in the Age to Come will his Name be revealed in the persons of the saints.[2] The Spirit refuses to speak of himself: it is his *métier*, rather, to impel human beings to receive the only-begotten Word who makes resonant the voice of the Father. Daringly, the *Catechism* speaks of this as a kind of kenosis of the Spirit, analogous to that of the Son in his Incarnation, and, we may add, that of the Father in originating the Word and, ultimately, in the Word the world.

---

[2]V. Lossky, *The Mystical Theology of the Eastern Church* (E.t. London 1957), p. 173. 'It is then that this divine Person, now unknown, not having his image in another hypostasis, will manifest himself in deified persons: the multitude of the saints will be his image.'

More than either of the other divine Persons, the Holy Spirit is known in and for what he does. The Father and the Son may be considered for their own sake, in abstraction from their work, though always by way of it, whereas, once we begin to think through the doctrine of the Spirit, we find his inner-Trinitarian being only in his communication of Father to Son, and Son to Father, so that even the name of his procession – spiration – is but a paraphrase of the title given to his person. So while it is a convenience of the order of exposition in the *Catechism* that the Spirit's eternal being (what the Greek Fathers would call his 'theology') has already been dealt with in the section on the Father, leaving over for consideration here only his mission to the world of time (his 'economy'), it happens to be the case that according, in this way, the lion's share of treatment to the works of the Holy Spirit chimes with the inner mystery of his person.

Of course there has never been a time when the Holy Spirit was *not* pursuing his saving work – any more than, in the famous rebuttal of the Arian attack on the Son, there was never a time when he was not, *simpliciter*. The being of the Most Holy Trinity, unlike that of Hegel's *Geist*, does not lie in its becoming. Nonetheless, such is the contrast between the Pentecostal gift of the Spirit and his presence and activity in the world prior to that crown and climax of the Paschal Mystery that, for the evangelist John, it almost seemed as if before then there was no Holy Spirit: *oupô gar ên Pneuma hagion*, 'It was not yet Holy Spirit' (John 7:39), a construction which has been compared to the English idiom for temporal seasons, as when we say 'It is not yet spring'. Only in the Last Days of the redemptive Incarnation is the Spirit's spring-time, his burgeoning presence, for only then, in the *Catechism's* words, is he 'revealed and given, recognised and welcomed', as a person.[3] And the consequence of the pouring out of the Holy Spirit into the body of the new humanity whose Head is Jesus Christ turns out to be those realities which are listed in the remaining formulae of the Creed: the holy Catholic Church, the communion of saints, the forgiveness of sins, the resurrection of the body, and

---

[3]Paragraph 686.

the life everlasting. The last portion of the historic Creeds is not, despite appearances, a shopping-list. These things are, in ordered and inter-related series, the fruits of the effusion of the Spirit of that Father and Son whose attributes and work have just been confessed.

The first of the Spirit-given realities to which the Creed bears witness is the Church. In exploring the significance of this fact, the *Catechism* shows itself as eager to maintain the bond, not only between pneumatology and Christology, but also between pneumatology and *ecclesiology*: doctrine about the Church. The deepest reason why, in the words of the Johannine Christ, the world cannot receive the Holy Spirit (cf. John 14:17), is that, were it to do so, it would have believed in the Son sent by the Father, and hence have ceased to be the world and become the Church instead. If the Holy Spirit is the locus – extended into the myriad human hypostases that he has made his dwelling – of communion with the Son, then the Church – which is also a multitude of personal subjects and yet, *au fond*, but one mystical 'person', the Bride of Christ – is the locus of communion with the Spirit. The *Catechism* lists eight ways in which the resources of the Church are thus pneumatic. The Spirit is found in the Church, firstly, in the Scriptures he has inspired – as no other literature in the world (or the Church, come to that!), for here he has been active in illuminating the minds of the sacred authors and directing their wills, to make of their literary materials a record of divine revelation to guide the Church until the Lord's Parousia. Then secondly, we have his presence in the living Tradition, that wider whole of faith and practice which is the proper ambience for the interpretation of Scripture. Here, consonant with its general view of fundamental theology, the *Catechism* treats the Fathers as the primary monuments of Tradition (from which, of course, it has already distinguished Scripture, which would otherwise occupy this exalted position). Next, the Spirit acts in the Church through her teaching-office which he 'assists'. Although in the patristic era the vocabulary of *inspiration* was by no means unknown for the deliverances of, especially, ecumenical Councils, with the soberly couched doctrine of the infallibility of the teaching-office (in its Petrine representative) promulgated at the First

Vatican Council the more tempered language of 'assistance' has become, as here, the norm. A third mediation of the Spirit in the Church is found in the liturgy of the sacraments, where by word and symbol the Holy Ghost places us in communion with Christ whose holy signs these are. If St Paul could speak in Romans of the Spirit himself praying in us, with sighs too deep for words (cf. Romans 8:26), then the foundation of the verbal praying of the members of the Church – whether by the outer word of vocal prayer, or the inner word of mental prayer – must be that same divine Person. After speaking, then, of these two forms of the Spirit's activity in the Church's prayer, liturgical and personal, the *Catechism* now mentions two forms of his self-gift in the work of the Church. One is internal, concerned with the building-up of the household of faith – and here what is at stake are 'charisms', like, for instance, those special impulses of the Spirit which have put a fair wind behind new Religious Orders or lay movements, and 'ministries', when, for example, devout members of the faithful offer their services as catechists of the young or of converts. The other is external, when the Church is spurred to communicate her faith to those outside, by means of apostolic and missionary activity. Lastly, and, as the vocabulary elected by the *Catechism* at this point would suggest, most importantly, the Spirit acts in the Church in those testimonies which are the lives of the saints. As his name, *Holy* Spirit, indicates, the Spirit is above all a Spirit of holiness, that divine Person who communicates to creatures a share in the uncreated Holy Being of God himself. Human holiness is the goal of the entire divine Economy *vis-à-vis* the world of man; hence it is in the saints above all that the Spirit accomplishes his mission of salvation.

While the Church, then, is the indispensable locus of our knowledge of the Holy Spirit and his ways, she herself cannot be grasped theologically – and so *as* the 'place' of the Spirit – except by a prior acceptance that the mission of the Spirit, distinct though inseparable from that of the Church, is a pre-condition of her making. The *Catechism* has already made this point,[4] but it seems worth underlining again. The Church does

[4]Ibid.

not enclose the Spirit. Rather does her mystery open out onto the Spirit's life. To say this is not to present a lower doctrine of the Church but a higher one: alone of human communities, in the Church the unsurpassable transcendence of the divine life is directly present to the world. A lesser God than this would also mean a lesser Church.

So far we have been dealing with the Trinitarian and ecclesiological *presuppositions* of the *Catechism's* pneumatology. When we turn to consider the *content* of its account of the Spirit, we find that it falls into five sections, which explore in turn: the intimate connexion between the Spirit's mission and the Son's; the symbols of the Spirit in Scripture; the rôle of the Spirit in the time before Christ, the age of the Promise; the time of Christ, time's fullness; and in the last times, where his mystery cannot be set forth without a simultaneous account of the destiny of the Church. In the prayer for the Parousia of the seer of the Apocalypse, it is the Spirit *and the Bride* who say 'Come'! (Apocalypse 22:17). It will readily be seen that all five of these topics concern, as predicted, the salvation-historical task of the Spirit, his 'economy'.

If, for the first great theologian of early Catholicism, Irenaeus of Lyons, the Son and the Spirit are the two hands of the Father, the *Catechism* repeats this claim in less imagistic language when it speaks of the 'conjoined mission' of the Spirit and the Son. Just as the eternal self-expression of the Father is – inseparably yet distinctly – the Son and the Spirit, so in that extension of the everlastingly fruitful generosity of the Father which is his saving plan for the world, we never find the Word in the absence of the Spirit, or the Spirit in splendid isolation from the Word. The work of Christ would have been impossible had not the Holy Spirit who rests on him from all eternity as the Son, informed his whole humanity in time. In the recuperative reflection of Johannine tradition, Jesus treats his own words as the 'words of God' only because of the unmeasured gift to him of the Holy Spirit (John 3:34). As the *Catechism* itself puts it, everything of salvific value that happens on the basis of the Incarnation 'derives from this fullness'.[5] At the same time, however, and

---

[5] Paragraph 690.

reflecting the order of the Trinitarian persons, where the Son is always named before the Spirit, the Son made man can and does send the Holy Spirit upon the disciples. Here the *Catechism* makes its own the Cappadocian exegesis which identifies the 'Glory' spoken of by Jesus in his High-Priestly Discourse with the Holy Spirit. The glorious Spirit the Father gives to his Christ, the Christ will in turn give to his disciples (cf. John 17:22). There is, then, a mutual conditioning of Son and Spirit in their respective economies. Nor is this contradictory: for the Spirit who proceeds from the Father precisely as the latter is Father of the Son, and so must be termed posterior – ontologically, not chronologically! – to the Word, is necessarily prior – both ontologically and chronologically – to the Word's assuming of our human nature, so that the Son in his humanity can only send the Spirit after the Spirit has enabled that humanity to be appropriated totally by the Word.

For all this Scripture has its own language, which is largely that not of metaphysics but of poetry. Just as in the sacraments God uses material things and gestures to communicate his gracious life, so in the images of the Bible he takes as his media their linguistic equivalents – verbal icons – to communicate his gracious truth. This befits our nature and situation. It bestows dignity on the material realities in whose setting we live, and helps reform our maladjusted attachment to images – for they are now used as means of grace.[6] When we think of the abuse of symbol and imagination found in the distortions of politics, the panderings of the entertainment and advertising industries to humanity's disordered fantasies, and the muddy stream which is our own interior imaginative life, we can be glad that the potent world-commanding and soul-cleansing symbols of Scripture have been given us. Thus, whereas for Scripture itself, as for the Liturgy and the classical theological language of the Church, the term 'Holy Spirit' must stand as the proper name of the Third in the Triune *taxis* or ordering, and while the Johannine, Pauline and Petrine traditions are acquainted with other 'appellations' whose symbolist content is either restrained (as with 'Paraclete', the Advocate or Counsellor), or

---

[6] Cf. Thomas Aquinas, *Summa Theologiae* IIIa., q. 67, a. 1.

non-existent (as with the 'Spirit of Christ', Romans 8:9, or 'the Spirit of the Lord', II Corinthians 3:17), the *Catechism* itself devotes much the greater part of its treatment of the pneumatological references of Scripture to the great symbols of water, oil, fire; cloud and light; the seal; the hand or finger, and last but not least, the dove. Very much in the spirit of the French Jesuit patristic scholar Jean Daniélou, whose studies of Jewish-Christian, Greek-Christian and Latin-Christian sources conspired to make him peculiarly sensitive to the importance of primitive Christian symbols in the early theology and sacramental practice of the Church, the *Catechism* weaves a tapestry of biblical and liturgical references in which to depict the multiform vitality the Spirit originates in the biblically founded experience of the Church.

The Spirit – never, then, without the Word, and both named and evoked in the inspired text of Scripture – acts in history after a fashion which the *Catechism* presents by means of a threefold periodisation. Its account of the Spirit's rôle in the 'time of the Promises', seen as inaugurated by the act of creation itself, is indebted, as so much in its treatment of the Creed, to the Greek Fathers. The Spirit who, in the words of a Byzantine troparion, ever 'keeps' the creation in the Father through the Son, was, by the Father's will, at work with the Son in the beginning to fashion man. The *Catechism* treats the history of humanity with the Spirit as tensed, in fact, between this primordial beginning and an equally constitutive ending. The key to the Spirit's rôle lies in the patristic analysis of the human animal as made to God's image, and in his likeness, or so the Book of Genesis reports. Although the Fathers do not entirely speak with one voice on this topic, the *Catechism* reproduces the predominant exegetical tradition among them when it describes fallen man as persisting in the image, but now deprived of the likeness, and links 'image' and 'likeness' here to Son and Spirit, respectively. The Son's redemptive work, on this view, is to repair the image, by exhibiting it in his own person, but to restore the likeness, by bestowing on human nature his 'Glory' – the Holy Spirit. Here, evidently, in the minds of the *Catechism's* makers, we have an example of the Fathers, by their exegetical work, playing a part in the communication of divine revelation by 'receiving' that revelation, in its scriptural record, in a particular way. Old Testament references to the Spirit of God – in the accounts of the theophanies and the Law, the hope of the Kingdom and the fact of the Exile, the promise of the Messiah and his sevenfold spirit as set forth in the Isaianic oracles – can thus be unified around one central theme: the making of a people whose humanity will be in God's image, to his likeness – which must mean, as Augustine showed in his profound discussion of the Trinitarian mirror in man – a humanity disposed to receive and be filled with the divine life it is called to reflect. The *Catechism* shows subtlety in its manipulation of the various biblical theologies involved. Presupposing as it does the unity of the Canon, it finds no difficulty in using those of the New Covenant to throw light on those of the Old. Thus for instance it links the Law to the Psalms via the exploration of the former's salvational rôle by Paul: just because the impossibility of keeping the whole Law brought about a deepened sense of sin, it also created an urgent desire for the Holy Spirit, to which the Book of Psalms attests. A similar unexpected turn awaits the careful reader in the account of the kingdom promised to David. Just because Israel (and Judah) chose to behave by normal political criteria, her sacred law, which should have been the sign of the covenant with Abraham and so the pledge of future blessings to mankind, ceased to provide the inner inspiration of her institutional existence. The Davidide monarchy thus had to be negated at the level of human action and affirmed on a new plane, that of the Holy Spirit, where it would belong not to the powerful but to those who are poor in spirit, that is, as the *Catechism* understands matters, 'poor according to the Spirit'.[7] Again, in the Exile the promises of God are broken according to the flesh, but kept according to the Spirit, as a purified remnant of Israel, reliant not on the historical process but on God alone, returns from Babylon to be 'one of the most transparent prefigurations of the Church'.[8] Echoing the 'joint mission' of Son and Spirit with

[7]Paragraph 709.
[8]Paragraph 710.

which this section of the *Catechism* opened, it finds in Israel's future hope two main lines of eschatological expectation, one centred on the Messiah, the other around a fresh outpouring of the Spirit, and sees both converge in the idea of a 'faithful remnant', raised up to receive its Messianic vindicator on whom the Spirit and his gifts will rest in unique abundance, and to initiate, through the Lord's Anointed, the 'last times' when the Spirit will renew hearts, reconcile peoples, and transform the created world into a sabbath of peace.

The economy of the Spirit in the age of the promise culminates in the shaping of this remnant, the *anawim* or poor of the Lord – humble and meek, awaiting the fulfilment of God's plan, expecting justice not from men but from God, and as such the 'master-work' of the Spirit's 'hidden mission'.[9] Their representatives are, in order of increasing significance, John the Baptist, Mary, and Jesus himself. It is to this triptych of figures that the *Catechism* devotes its account of the Holy Spirit in the 'fullness of time'. This is not a matter of repeating what has already been said about the Precursor, our Lady and the Lord Jesus himself, but of tracing the rôle of the Holy Spirit in their regard. In John the Spirit finalises his task of forming a people prepared for the divine visitation. He is the icon of the Spirit: announcing the consolation of Israel, he appears as the voice of the Comforter who is coming, and whose work of testifying to the Light – the 'Light from Light, very God from very God', of the Creed – he anticipates. In blessed Mary, thanks to the Spirit's preparation, at the heart of the faithful remnant, of a perfect Daughter of Zion, the Father finds a dwelling place for his Son where the Spirit too will take up his abode. The *Catechism* recalls the sophiologists – most commonly found among the Russian theologians but by no means unknown in the Latin West – who have seen in Mary a figure of the divine Wisdom, for the Word and the Spirit dwell within her. In five ways does Mary stand out as the Spirit's work of art. She is graciously prepared by him to be of all creatures the most capable of receiving the ineffable Godhead. Through him she realises the Father's plan, as the Spirit's power makes her

[9] Paragraph 716.

consecrated virginity fruitful in a divine motherhood. By her, the Spirit manifests the only Son of the Father, as she is made the 'burning bush of the definitive theophany'.[10] Through her, the Spirit begins to place others in communion with Christ, since it is only by relation to the Mother, initially, that others – the shepherds, the magi, Symeon and Anna – can recognise the Son. Finally, at Pentecost, when the mission of the Spirit at the mid-point of saving history reaches its climax, Mary becomes the new Eve, Mother of all living in Christ.

One would hardly expect an account of Jesus and the Spirit to be more concise than a theological comment on the Spirit and the Mother of Christ. But the *Catechism* must beware of merely repeating itself, since its Christology has already paid close attention to the pneumatological aspects of the life of Jesus. Here it chooses to concentrate on the relation of the Spirit to the Son within the complex moment which is the Death and Resurrection of the Lord: only when thanks to his victorious Sacrifice Jesus is himself bathed in the glory of the Spirit can he fully reveal the Spirit. By condensing into a few lines all the Johannine references to the work of the Paraclete in the Last Supper Discourse, the *Catechism* attempts to evoke the difference of mode in which the Spirit is present in the world after the Atonement, as compared with before. And when the risen Christ gives the Spirit to the disciples, *pari passu* with their marching orders as his apostles, the 'mission of Christ and the Spirit becomes the mission of the Church'[11] – a statement which begins the gentle elision from pneumatology to ecclesiology in the *Catechism's* pages.

Pentecost is, after all, both the revelation of the Spirit as, precisely, Spirit of Father and Son, and, at the same time, the birthday of the Church. The *Catechism* insists on a relatively 'realised' eschatology, whereby the Kingdom is not for us simply future, but is already present, thanks to the extraordinary events of those few weeks – from the Paschal *triduum* to Pentecost – which changed the world. It proposes the claims of realised eschatology in two ways. One concerns theological

---

[10] Paragraph 724.
[11] Paragraph 730.

epistemology: on the first Pentecost, the mystery of the Holy Trinity was fully revealed – though we have noted that the hypostasis of the Spirit is not yet directly disclosed in history. Less conditionally warranted is the *Catechism's* second relevant claim, made in terms, rather, of soteriology: from Pentecost on, the Kingdom proclaimed by Christ is thrown open to those who believe in him such that here and now they can share in the inner-Trinitarian life. Here the *Catechism* makes its own the wonderful troparian of the Byzantine Vespers for Pentecost, used in the post-Communion prayers of the Liturgy of St John Chrysostom:

> We have seen the true Light, we have received the heavenly Spirit, we have found the true faith: we adore the indivisible Trinity, who has saved us.

Though much modern Catholic theology has tended, since the Second Vatican Council, towards a more 'consequent' eschatology, notably by increasing the distance between the Kingdom and the Church, the wholesale repudiation of realised eschatology would turn Christians into no more than Jews who happen to know the name of the Messiah. The high doctrine of the Church and the ministry, the sacraments and the Liturgy, the Mother of God and the saints, in Catholicism all require the maintenance of an eschatology with a strongly realised component.

The *Catechism* closes its pneumatological section by considering the effect, on both the personal and the communitarian levels, of the outpouring of the Spirit of Christ in Pentecostal grace. Recalling that, in Latin theology, one of the titles given the Spirit is *Amor*, 'love', the effect of his effusion on individual persons can be charted from the text in Romans where Paul hymns the love of God as 'poured into our hearts by the Holy Spirit who has been given to us' (Romans 5:5). Since through sin all men are wounded stragglers, the first result of pneumatic charity must be the forgiveness of sins, which comes about through baptismal communion in the Holy Spirit. We should expect Love to forgive sins; it is his avocation. Secondly, the guilty but forgiven ones receive the Spirit as the pledge or first fruits of a further inheritance – the eternal life of the Trinity which is itself love. The Spirit's title serves also to describe the relations of communion between Father, Son and Spirit. It is because the Holy Ghost is the bond of unity of Father and Son that he can be called 'Love'. And thirdly, if charity is the principle of our new life in Christ, then the fruits that the Spirit produces on the Vine of Jesus are necessarily cognate with love itself – the joy, peace, patience, kindness, goodness, faithfulness, gentleness, and self-control listed in the Letter to the Galatians as a word-portrait of the Christian life (Galatians 5:25).

The *Catechism* connects pneumatology with the divine plan for the corporate life of humankind – with ecclesiology – by means of the concept of *mission*. The joint mission of Son and Spirit is continued in a social organism which is at once the Son's (ecclesial) body and the Spirit's temple. The addition of the Church's sending to those of Spirit and Son does not make a twosome into a threesome, for the Church is the sacrament of their conjoined mission, not its supplement. A glimpse of the fundamentally missionary spirit in which the *Catechism* will approach its treatise on ecclesiology is at once available: the Church, in the image of the Spirit, exists by announcing the work of the Son, and testifying to him, so as to spread everywhere the mystery of participation in the Trinitarian life.

Before plunging into these waters, however, the *Catechism* pauses to look ahead to the three sub-books which will follow on its commentary on the Creed, linking each to the economy of the Spirit. The *Catechism's* treatise on the *sacraments* will portray Christ as communicating the sanctifying Spirit to the Church's members by these sacred signs. Its study of the *commandments* will present Christian ethical existence as new life in Christ according to the Spirit. And lastly, its accounts of spirituality and prayer will treat the Holy Spirit – and no human teacher – as *the* Master of prayer *par excellence*.

The German philosopher-theologian Romano Guardini prophesied that the twentieth century would be the 'century of the Church' in Catholic theology. And in point of fact, many of the themes of the ecclesiology of the past have been retrieved by a process of *recursus ad fontes*, related to each other in illuminating ways, and occasionally extended on the basis of genial insights from Scripture, Tradition and the questions put to the patrimony of Christian believing from the contemporary cultures in which the churches of the *Catholica* live out their life. No finer summary of the best in the contemporary ecclesiological renascence can be found than *Lumen Gentium*, the Dogmatic Constitution of the Second Vatican Council on the Church. Wisely, the *Catechism* treats that document as its guide, while also contributing a modest originality of its own at certain points.

This combination of fidelity to the Conciliar masterpiece and yet willingness to adopt a changed angle of vision is immediately apparent in the preamble to the *Catechism's* ecclesiology. On the one hand, by citing, and explaining, the opening words of *Lumen Gentium* – which proclaim *Christ (not the Church, as is often mis-remembered!)* as the Light of all peoples, the *Catechism's* authors are able to make the point that the doctrine of the Church is properly dependent on Christology: the Church cannot be understood save in relation to the mission of the Son. On the other hand, by treating ecclesiology in the context of an interpretation of the Catholic Creeds, the *Catechism* is ineluctably led to balance this christological reference of the Council by a pneumatological allusion of its own – since the series of *credenda* which open by mentioning 'the holy Catholic Church' are governed by the clause 'I [or 'we'] believe in the Holy Spirit'. The doctrine of the Church is properly dependent on pneumatology: the Church cannot be understood save in relation to the mission of the Spirit.

The *Catechism* incorporates seven basic approaches to this topic. *First,* as with its treatment of the Holy Spirit, it assembles *the names of, and symbols for, the Church,* as found in Tradition and (above all) Scripture. Unlike *Lumen Gentium,* it sets at the head of these a single key ecclesiological concept: the Church as the divine convocation of human beings into God's presence – at first, at the foot of Sinai, where Israel received the Torah and became the Lord's holy people, but now, in the context of the *Catholica,* to the ends of the earth. While insisting on the inseparability of the three human configurations which the term 'church' can bear in Scripture and Tradition – the liturgical assembly, the local church and the Church universal, the *Catechism*, rightly, gives priority, albeit discreetly, to the last. For the symbolic theology of the scriptural images for the Church which follows – the sheepfold, field or vineyard, building and temple, spouse – the text plunders unashamedly the sixth chapter of *Lumen Gentium*. Only when an initial definition of the Church – however sketchy – has been presented, and the contours of the reality to which that concept applies further evoked by a rehearsal of the images that cluster around it, does the *Catechism* proceed with its account of *the Church in the plan of God* – the *second* of its approaches. Placed first in the Conciliar Constitution, the authors of the *Catechism* may well have thought it pedagogically preferable to begin, constrastingly, with a stab at defining the Church – not least since in the thirty years which separate the opening of the Second Vatican Council from the promulgation of the *Catechism*, secularism and the decline of doctrinal instructedness among Catholic Christians have taken their toll. Although, as befits a salvation-historical account of the Church, the *Catechism's* comments on her rôle in the divine plan proceed chronologically rather than thematically, the deeper structure of its teaching at this juncture is Trinitarian. The 'Church in the plan of God' means: the Church as conceived in the heart of the Father, instituted by the Son, manifested by the Holy Spirit. Especially striking – and a novelty in comparison with *Lumen Gentium* – is the stress on protology: the simultaneous origination, at any rate in the divine will, of the Church and the world. Here the *Catechism* gathers together a number of texts from the early Greek Fathers and ecclesiastical writers – Hermas, Aristides, Justin, Epiphanius – which find in the Church the goal of the world, that for which the world was made. We shall not be far wrong in ascribing the retrieval of these texts to a desire to re-emphasise the mysteric nature of the Church, dear to Eastern Orthodoxy, and obscured in the predominantly sociological thinking of many contemporary Western Catholics. The sections which follow on the Son's institution of the Church in time, and the Spirit's manifestation of what the Son has founded both in time and in the meta-historical dimension of the Age to Come, add little to the account already given of the ecclesiological initiatives of Son and Spirit when those divine persons were the focus of attention. However, by closing its salvation-historical treatment of the Church with the Church in glory, the *Catechism* succeeds rather better than *Lumen Gentium* in showing that the eschatological Church is none other than the present Church *in fieri*, in becoming.

The *Catechism's* third approach is to tackle 'head on' the subject of *the Church as mystery*, and to show that, with the aid of the ancient concept of *sacramentum* – whose most obvious, but by no means exclusive, application is found in the seven sacraments, the mysteric character of the Church is in no way separated from its societal, and therefore institutional, substance. Just as Jesus in his High Priestly Prayer petitioned that the disciples might be in the world but not of it, the *Catechism* declares the Church to be in history and yet to transcend it. Treating the Church as a theandric – divine-human – reality, is not to ignore the ignoble deeds whereby she has been diminished by unworthy members. Making its own an audacious text from St Bernard's commentary on the Song of Songs, which synthesises the most laudatory statements about the Church with others bordering on the vituperative, for the Bride of the Canticle is 'black, yet comely' (Song of Songs 1:5), the *Catechism* reflects the mediaeval commentator's sense of proportion: though the fatigue and troubles of a lengthy exile weary her, the Church is (more primordially) adorned with the very beauty of heaven. So as to avoid all possible *entrée* to horizontalism – which would regard the Church as a kind of sacred version of the United Nations Organisation on the macro-level, and a good neighbourhood scheme on the micro, it roundly asserts her to be a mystery of the union of human beings with God, leaving no hostages to fortune by omitting to add, in this context, 'and each other'. The *Catechism* will not fail to make that second statement in due course, but it prefixes this uncompromisingly theocentric assertion. Moreover, reflecting the bridal mysticism of Tradition, powerfully revived in the modern period by Balthasar, it stresses that the Church can be called a 'mystery' in her own right only because of her nuptial union with her Bridegroom, Jesus Christ. Especially Balthasarian, though drawn more immediately from *Mulieris dignitatem*, the letter of Pope John Paul II on women in the Church, is the notion that the Church's Marian dimension takes precedence over her Petrine–spiritual motherhood, over the fatherhood of office – precisely because it is Mary, not Peter, who embodies the Church as divine Bride.

The Church, then, on this third approach, is what we may call a 'subordinate mystery'. She mediates the superordinate mystery of the union of human beings with God, thanks to her abiding possession of the grace of sponsal union with the Son. Yet her own mystery is in turn mediated by those visible aspects of her being, deriving from her divine-human Head, which signify or express in sacramental guise the subordinate mystery itself. That sacramental structure comprises all the constitutive dimensions of her visible existence – for in Baptism and Confirmation her laity is made, just as in Order her ministers are set aside for sacred duties. The aim of all her visible activity – from ritual to acts of governance – is *holiness* (citing once again the papal letter on women). This follows inevitably from the *Catechism's* presentation of the sacramental structure of the Church as a sign of the subordinate mystery – the Church as Bride of Christ, itself ordered to the superordinate mystery – the union of men with God. It is because such union is the indispensable basis of all abiding harmony between human individuals and groups that the *Catechism* – its primary point now unmistakably established – can go on to speak of the Church as, in the second place, the sign of the unity of the race itself. If, then, the *Catechism* shows a certain tendency at this juncture somewhat to marginalise what Cardinal Henri de Lubac, in his *Catholicisme*, termed the 'social aspects of dogma'[12] – for, as we have seen, it wishes to affirm the unconditional primacy of the theocentric, and of sanctity – it turns in the end as if by compensation to the Apocalypse, with its vision of a city where every nation, race, people and tongue praise God and the Lamb (Apocalypse 7:9), in order to retrieve a theme

---

[12]H. de Lubac, *Catholicisme. Les aspects sociaux du dogme* (Paris 1938).

important to the Council though there too mentioned only second:

> By her relationship with Christ, the Church is a kind of sacrament or sign of intimate union with God *and of the unity of all mankind.*[13]

The *fourth* of the *Catechism's* ecclesiological approaches is a *Trinitarian theology of the Church* – as explicitly Trinitarian as its second was implicitly so. The Church is the people of the Father, the body of the Son, the temple of the Holy Ghost. The 'people of God' motif and its treatment are indebted to *Lumen Gentium*, which likewise takes the term as synonymous with the royal and prophetic priesthood of all believers – though here the *Catechism's* comments are supported by an extended passage from the sermons of Leo the Great, rather than, as with the conciliar text, by references to the Pian popes, and notably the eleventh and twelfth of that name. By disengaging this central topic in First Peter's notion of the messianic people (cf. I Peter 2:9–10) from other sub-themes adjoined by *Lumen Gentium* the *Catechism* confers on it a clearer profile. At the same time, the subjects thus bracketed – and notably the relation of particular or diocesan churches to the Church universal, and the sense in which a host of categories of non-Catholics, ranging from other Christians, through the adherents of non-Christian religions, to out-and-out unbelievers, may be said to be linked to this unique sacral people – will have to be dealt with somewhere. As we shall see, the *Catechism* locates them, suitably enough, under the heading of the *catholicity* of the Church.

If all the Church's members share in the threefold office of the Messiah as priest, prophet and king, then they carry the burden likewise of the responsibilities which attend these charges. *Noblesse oblige.* The prophetic office is discharged primarily in adhering faithfully to the revelation once given to the saints, deepening one's understanding of it, and testifying to it – which means, above all, to *Christ* – in the midst of the world. The royal office is carried out by serving Christ, notably in the poor and suffering of the world. The *Catechism* speaks

---

[13] *Lumen Gentium* 1. Italics added.

more allusively about the priestly office, in part no doubt because its duties will be developed at much fuller length later, in the sections of the *Catechism* on the sacraments and on prayer. The quasi-identification of the 'people of God' notion with that of the priestly, prophetic and royal community of the Messiah may seem to make it *a priori* unlikely that this ecclesiological theme could degenerate either into the false democratism of a political theology or into a neo-Judaic, and purely Old Testament, comprehension of a holy people. These are, however, the by no means unfounded criticisms lodged by two such influential makers of the conciliar ecclesiology as Cardinal Ratzinger and Père Congar. Hence the greater prominence given in the *Catechism* to the Christological and pneumatological themes which now follow: the Church is not only the people of the Father, but the body of the Son and the temple of the Spirit: here biological and cultic analogies displace the politological one of 'people'. If the French poet and social commentator Charles Péguy could utilise the paired terms of *politique* and *mystique* to contrast two views, one superficial, one profound, of human solidarity, then the *Catechism*, as it progresses from people of the Father through body of the Son to temple of the Spirit accentuates a *mystical* inflexion. The comparison of the Church to the body, with Christ as its head, makes it clear that the redeemed people is not only gathered *around* Christ, but is also united *in him*.[14] Baptismal communion in the death and Resurrection of the Lord is intensified by eucharistic communion where those who are 'in Christ' through Baptism are concorporated into his embodied life in its abiding condition of accepted sacrificial outpouring before the Father. Numerous texts of all periods, assembled by modern practitioners of 'eucharistic ecclesiology', testify to the soundness of the intuition here presented.[15]

---

[14]Paragraph 789.
[15]Some are laid out in my *Theology in the Russian Diaspora. Church, Fathers, Eucharist in Nikolai Afanas'ev, 1893–1966* (Cambridge 1989), pp. 163–176; see also P. McPartlan, *The Eucharist Makes the Church: Henri de Lubac and John Zizioulas in Dialogue* (Edinburgh 1993).

Eucharistic union, even at the mystical heart penetrated by those worshippers who receive with perfect dispositions, never cancels out, however, the diversity of those thus united. 'I love, therefore we are', is the Catholic – and more specifically the eucharistic – version of the Cartesian *cogito*. The unity with Christ which belonging to his body implies is a differentiated unity, and depending on whether emphasis is laid on the unitive or the differentiating aspect Christ himself will be symbolised in this ecclesiology either as Head or as Bridegroom. The *Catechism* insists that, in the 'total Christ' – Augustine's phrase for Head and members combined – Christ does not so much crown his people by being head as make them his instrument, using them to extend through the universe that 'primacy' which the Letter to the Colossians (1:18) accords him. Again, Christ does not marry his Bride so as to subject her to his whim but – following this time Paul's Corinthian correspondence – in order that, united with him, his members may 'become one spirit with him' (I Corinthians 6:15–17; cf. II Corinthians 11:2). This is subtle, for each symbolism – the unitive symbol of the Head, the relational symbol of the Husband – catches fire, at the *Catechism*'s hands, from the other, thus suggesting their point of convergence in a reality – Christ-and-the-Church – which, as a unique union, finally escapes all categories and images.

The deepest level of *mystique* in the *Catechism's* professedly Trinitarian theology of the Church is, however, that of the Spirit's temple. Citing the sermons of Augustine, the Holy Spirit is the soul – the seat of consciousness – of the body of Christ. No wonder that Irenaeus, in his own pneumatic ecclesiology in the *Adversus Haereses*, could call the Spirit in the Church not only the pledge of incorruptibility for Christ's Spouse but also a 'ladder for ascending to God'. And yet, if the Holy Spirit is the soul of the Church's body his presence must also be relevant to her public exteriority of action, and not just to her secret interiority of communion with Father and Son. The soul, after all, is a principle of life and activity as well as of inmost identity and reflection. And so, at the conclusion of its Trinitarian ecclesiology in miniature, the *Catechism* returns to the forum of the action of Christians, treating of the

Professing the Faith: The Creed on the Holy Spirit   119

uncovenanted gifts or 'charisms' of the Spirit, found among persons of every walk of life, and ranging from the commonplace to the spectacular. All such pneumatic charismata, the *Catechism* insists, 'directly or indirectly benefit the Church, ordered as they are to her building up, to the good of men and to needs of the world'.[16] The same integration of inner and outer elements, all set within the context of a view of the Church as the creation of the Trinity, is beautifully expressed in the *Pentecoste* of the early nineteenth century Italian poet Alessandro Manzoni. The latter, after briefly introducing the Church as the Church of the living Father, goes on to describe her birth from the side of the Redeemer, and manifestation by the Pentecostal Spirit:

> Mother of the saints; image of the heavenly city; perpetual guardian of the ever-living Blood; you that for so many centuries have suffered, fought and prayed; that set up your tents from sea to sea;

> realm of those who hope; Church of the living God; where were you? what dark corner received you at your birth, when your King, drawn by villains up the hill to die, encrimsoned the clods of his sublime altar?

> And then, the sacred body now issued from the dark, when he breathed in the power of the new life; and when, the price of our pardon in his hands, he rose from this dust to the Father's throne;

> you, who suffering had watched him suffer, aware of the mysteries of his being, you, deathless daughter of his victory, where were you? Awake to nothing but your fears, safe alone in being forgotten, you stayed in seclusion and secrecy until that sacred day,

> when upon you the renewing Spirit descended, and kindled in your right hand the ever-burning torch; when

---

[16]Paragraph 799.

as a beacon for the nations he placed you on the mountain,
and on your lips set flowing the fountain of speech ...[17]

The *fifth* ecclesiological avenue explored by the *Catechism* looks at *the four 'marks' of the Church*, as named in the Nicene–Constantinopolitan Creed: 'one, holy, catholic and apostolic Church'. The *Catechism* insists on two points from the outset: first, these four attributes are inseparable – and here it cites a letter of 1864 on the Anglican branch theory from the predecessor of the present Congregation for the Doctrine of the Faith to the Catholic bishops of England and Wales; and secondly, they identify features belonging at once to the Church *and to her mission*, thus picking up again the strong emphasis on the missionary action of the Church which originally formed, at the junction of pneumatology and ecclesiology, the link between those two great regions of doctrinal believing in the *Catechism's* overall scheme.

The *Catechism* distinguishes, in effect, between the sources of the Church's *unity*, which are in every sense divine, and the means whereby her unity is guarded and fostered, which are divinely founded but work by way of human means. The ultimate source of the Church's unity is the Holy Trinity, whose own inter-personal communion she reflects on earth. To this thought, especially vital to the influential ecclesiology of the North African doctor Cyprian, two further considerations, owed to the documents of the Second Vatican Council, are appended. The mediate sources of the Church's unity lie in the missions of the Son and the Spirit, for, as *Gaudium et Spes* – the Pastoral Constitution on the Church in the Modern World – affirmed, the Church is one through the universally reconciling work of the Word Incarnate, while, as *Unitatis redintegratio* – the Conciliar Decree on Ecumenism – pointed out, the Holy Spirit is her inner principle of unity. The makers of the *Catechism* have found a superb text from Clement of Alexandria with which to unify these materials, for it explicitly links the one

---

[17]A. Manzoni, 'Pentecoste', in A. Chiari and F. Ghisalberti (ed.), *Opere di Alessandro Manzoni: I. Poesie e tragedie* (Milan 1957); the English translation is by Fr Kenelm Foster, O.P., of Blackfriars, Cambridge, in *Comparative Criticism. A Year Book 3* (1981), pp. 203–205.

Father, one Logos, one Spirit with the single 'virgin become mother, and I should like to call her "Church"'. But what are the means whereby Father, Son and Spirit engender unity in the community of the redeemed? After naming charity as the first of these, the *Catechism* lists those other 'bonds of unity' which theological tradition, not least at the Second Vatican Council, and in its canonical step-child, the code of canons of the Latin Church, has identified. And these are: unity in a single faith; unity in worship, notably through sharing the same sacraments; and unity in the social life of the Church governed as that is by the successors of the apostles of Jesus Christ. It is because the continuing identity of the apostolic college cannot be located without reference to its primatial head, the successor of Peter, that communion with the Roman pope is essential to unity, that constitutive mark of the Church as Christ willed her to be.

That is not to say that the Church is meant to be a homogeneous monolith. Diversity, though not a theological mark of the Church, has certainly always been one of her features: the sheer profusion of the gifts of God in revelation and salvation, as well as the differences between human individuals and groups guarantee that. Once those differences are baptised into the mystery of a Church possessed of the incalculable riches of the revealing and saving Word, the result is the precious pluralism of the various particular churches. (How much poorer the Church would be deprived of either its Eastern or its Western 'lung'!) This is not to say, however, that a lighthearted cry of *Vive la différence* solves all problems. As the *Catechism* points out, sin can turn the good of diversity into the evil of heresy, apostasy and schism; legitimate pluralism can degenerate (as indeed the history of post-conciliar Catholicism demonstrates) into anarchy. In the past this phemonenon has bequeathed the historic schisms which have ruptured the unity of Christendom – to which 'wounds to unity' the *Catechism* shows itself most sensitive. It echoes *Unitatis redintegratio* in finding outside the single Church's visible unity numerous elements of evangelical truth and apostolic order, such that the tragically separated Churches and ecclesial communities (the difference between the two turns on the presence or absence of a ministerial and thus sacramental life in the apostolic succession) can be instruments used by the Spirit of Christ for man's salvation. At the same time, and once again in keeping with the Conciliar decree, the *Catechism* does not treat these 'elements' as autonomous and free-floating; rather do they derive from the fullness of gracious truth Christ has given his holy Catholic Church, and coming from that source, carry a built-in gravitational pull back – or on! – towards the Church's unity.

This is the dogmatic basis, therefore, on which an ecumenical optimism may be constructed even when, in terms of empirical history, the future looks bleak indeed. Under the heading 'Towards unity', the *Catechism* rehearses the authentic principles of Catholic ecumenism – as distinct from an inauthenticity of indifference, whether *vis-à-vis* the reunion of Christians itself or in regard to the inalienable fullness of doctrine held in trust for others by the dogmatic magisterium of the Catholic Church. Nor is there any backtracking on the Council's generosity towards separated Christians when the *Catechism* gives priority to a spiritual ecumenism of abiding renewal, continual conversion and prayer, rather than the professional ecumenism of specialist formation, bilateral dialogue and sectorial cooperation on agreed projects with other churches. That is the order given in *Unitatis redintegratio* itself, and its wisdom is evident. Without an efflorescence of the specifically Catholic dogmata in spiritual living on the one side, and a change of optic on the other, no amount of talk or even action will avail to persuade non-Catholics into affirming the beautiful truth of what, historically, their communities have vehemently denied.

The Church, after all, is not only one; she is also *holy*: her second 'mark'. Inasmuch as Jesus Christ, whom the *Gloria* of the Western Mass salutes as 'the only Holy One', has embraced her as his Spouse, the Church is necessarily affected by this unique contact with the infinite holiness of the divine Trinity, whose Mediator he is. Owing to her union with him, she is not only all-hallowed but all-hallowing, the agent of sanctification as well as its recipient. All her activities converge on human sanctification and the doxological praise of the God who has shared his holiness with men – as the Conciliar Constitution on the Sacred Liturgy declares.

So far as her individual faithful are concerned, such is the war of sin with grace in our members that such holiness is far from complete in us *as persons*. Nonetheless each and every one is called to be perfect, and furnished, in the life of the Church, with all the necessary means to hand for becoming so. The *Catechism* treats charity as the 'soul' of holiness; as in the theology of morals-under-grace of St Thomas Aquinas, charity unifies the virtues in view of their common end, union through Christ with God in the beatific vision. Citing St Thérèse of Lisieux's *Histoire d'une âme*: as the heart of the mystical Body of Christ, charity is co-extensive with the call of God to human destiny, despite the latter's innumerable concrete forms. And if, when contemplating the many counter-forms that lovelessness can take, the faithful Christian is depressed at the thought of the tares which grow within Christ's field, the *Catechism* provides grounds for encouragement in rounding off its section on the Church's holiness with a mention of the canonised saints, and, at their centre, the Mother of God. Solemn canonisation of those whose lives have shown forth heroic charity is a recognition by the Church of the power of the Spirit of holiness and a motive of hope for all believers. And as for Mary, in her the Church's deepest nature is already radiantly apparent, for she is the *Panaghia*, the all-holy Virgin. The *Catechism of the Catholic Church* could well have cited here as a pithy summary the much-traduced *Catechism of Christian Doctrine* known colloquially in England as the 'Penny Catechism', which offers on this subject an admirable formula:

> The Church is holy because she teaches a holy doctrine, offers to all the means of holiness, and is distinguished by the eminent holiness of so many thousands of her children.[18]

Actually, more will be said on this topic when the new *Catechism* reaches the seventh and last of its ecclesiological perspectives, looking at the clause of the Creed on the Church from the angle of its successor clause, on the communion of saints.

---

[18] *A Catechism of Christian Doctrine, as Approved by the Archbishops and Bishops of England and Wales, and Directed by Them to be Used in all their Dioceses* (Ditchling, Sussex, 1931), Paragraph 96.

This one, holy Church is also *catholic*. It is a theological commonplace that catholicity may be understood of the Church either qualitatively – as a statement about the integral nature of her faith and its capacity to meet human need, or quantitatively, as an expression of her world-wide mission. The *Catechism* places its emphasis firmly on the first of these. What is unusual is the decision to treat the holistic – *kath' holon* – quality of the Church's hold on divine revelation, and thus healing and sanctifying power for human life – in such determinedly *christocentric* terms. The Church is qualitatively catholic only because in her *Christ* is present. If the Church is, as the Writer to the Ephesians has it, 'his body, the fullness of him who fills all in all' (Ephesians 1:22–23), then she must have received fully, totally, and so in a catholic fashion, all the means of salvation the Redeemer has to give. In this sense, the Church was already catholic in unsurpassable fashion while still gathered in the Cenacle, at the first Pentecost. The second sense of catholicity, quantitative or geographical catholicity, is only applied to her, by contrast, when, impelled by the Spirit, her apostles tumble out of the Upper Room onto the streets of Jerusalem, and go forth through Judaea and Samaria into all the world – as the Acts of the Apostles will have it, by cutting off its narrative on the outskirts of that Rome to which (and therefore *from* which) all roads lead.

With this statement all that is important on the Church's catholic character could be considered spoken. But the *Catechism* lingers on the topic for two reasons. First, it has unfinished business to deal with: the topics of the universal Church and the particular churches, and the belonging to the Church of those not visibly her members, which were earlier left aside in an effort to improve the *ordo expositionis* of the ecclesiology of *Lumen Gentium*. Since Christ is present in all legitimate local gatherings of the faithful, around their bishops, with their presbyters and deacons in *corona*, the *Catechism* can hardly deny to the particular churches the title of qualitatively catholic. However, it insists that they are *fully* catholic only on account of their communion with that one particular church which is the nexus of their inter-relations, their lovers' knot, the church of Rome which, in the pregnant phrase of Ignatius of

Antioch's *Letter to the Romans*, 'presides in charity' – or, better, perhaps, as a rendering of the Greek, 'presides in the Charity', in the love-circle of all the churches. A passage from Pope Paul VI's apostolic exhortation *Evangelii nuntiandi* makes clear that this affirmation is intended as a warning against any federalist misconstruing of the nature of the Church as communion – a theme also taken up in the 1992 Letter of the Congregation for the Doctrine of the Faith *On Some Aspects of the Church as Communion* where we read:

> The particular churches, insofar as they are part of the one Church of Christ, have a special relationship of mutual interiority with the whole, that is, with the universal Church, because in every particular church, the one, holy, catholic and apostolic Church of Christ is truly present and active. For this reason, the universal Church cannot be conceived as the sum of the particular churches, or as a federation of particular churches. That Church is not the result of the communion of the churches, but is, in its essential mystery, a reality ontologically and temporally prior to every individual particular church.[19]

It is the vocation of the (particular) church of Rome to represent, precisely, this anteriority of the Church universal to the particular churches. Since the universal Church, considered apart from the particular churches, is not a possible subject of historical action, the particular church whose bishop is simultaneously the universal primate acts for it in this regard.

The matter of, Who belongs to the Catholic Church? cannot be so summarily disposed of, for it raises vast questions about the relation of the true religion to other faiths, and indeed to men and women of no faith at all. For Catholicism, the Church is, under Christ, the constitutive, though not the exclusive, way of salvation. The Church exists so as to perpetuate Christ's redeeming work, equipped for this task as she is by her apostolic heritage of faith, sacraments and ministry, together with the promised assistance of the risen Christ, who acts through the gift of the Holy Spirit. Accordingly, the Church is,

---
[19]Congregation for the Doctrine of the Faith, *Letter to the Bishops of the Catholic Church on some aspects of the Church understood as Communion* (E.t. London 1992), p. 9.

as *Lumen Gentium*, and other documents of the Second Vatican Council put it, the 'universal sacrament of salvation'; she is also, in the words of Pope John Paul II's encyclical *Redemptoris Mater*, the 'first beneficiary of salvation', since Christ won her for himself at the cost of his own blood. Ever since Pentecost, the ordinary way of salvation is through believing in the Gospel, and incorporation in the Gospel community. To be incorporated fully in that Church it is necessary to be a baptised Christian in union with the bishops in communion with the pope – in a word, a Catholic. Such incorporation in the Church involves, positively, maintenance of three 'bonds' – profession of faith, sacramental participation, and shepherding by lawful pastors, as well as, negatively, not being in a condition of legitimate excommunication on account of grave sins. And yet even Catholics who sing in these chains of ecclesial communion fail to be one with the Church at the deepest level if they do not also possess the indwelling Gift of the Holy Spirit. Indeed, unless they persevere in charity they will not even be saved. This possibility of belonging to the Church's body but not to her heart raises the question of whether one may belong to her heart without belonging to her body.

Now we have already seen, in the context of the ecclesial mark of unity, that, thanks to their possession of some of the divinely instituted means of grace, the Catholic Church can be said to operate through schismatic, or partially schismatic, churches and ecclesial communities. The *Catechism*, after reaffirming this point, turns to the more delicate area of whether and how non-Christians may be described as ordered to the true Church by what Pope Pius XII called an 'unconscious will and desire'. So far as the Jewish people are concerned, the *Catechism* finds that they are related to the Catholic Church not only by the enduring validity of the promises made them under the Old Covenant, but also owing to the 'analogy' which holds between their future hope and that of the new and universal people of God. Both expect the Messiah, though the latter not only knows his name but awaits him in the glorious manifestation of a *second* coming. And as to Islam, Muslims may be said to enjoy a special relation to the Church both by sharing in the Abrahamic revelation of Genesis (Judaism, Christianity, Islam, are the three Abrahamic faiths) and by looking to the future determination of all history which is the last and general Judgment – though unlike both Christians and Jews, Muslims are unaware that its human executive is the Messiah. What can be said of the non-Abrahamic religions, whether those of the great religious cultures of South Asia and the Far East, or the more lowly life-ways of the so-called 'traditional' religions of less complex societies? Their relation to the Church can only be the highly indirect one that is mediated by the possession of a common humanity, where the one God is both the source and the goal, Creator and final Redeemer. And while recognising that in (for example) such religions there may be integrable values which serve as a *praeparatio evangelica*, these elements of the good and the true are intermixed with others more malign and deceitful. Since the Conciliar Declaration on Non-Christian Religions, *Nostra aetate*, confined itself of set purpose to what Catholics and various categories of non-Christians might be said to have in common, the impression has gained ground (though to be sure other Conciliar texts, cited in this context by the *Catechism*, could have scotched it) that the world religions were treated by the Council as ordinary means of salvation for their practitioners – with lamentable consequences for the theory and practice of mission. The *Catechism* takes the opportunity to correct this misapprehension. It presents a brief catena of patristic texts on the Church as the unique locus of divine-human unity and salvation, the 'reconciled world' of Augustine, the Ark of salvation of other Fathers too numerous to name. Outside her, indeed, there is no salvation: that is, positively understood, as the *Catechism* has it, all grace flows through the Church-body from Christ her Head. Christ's universal mediation of grace, while it excludes parallel or complementary mediation by other agents, does not exclude participated forms of mediation that gain their value from his own mediatorial work. And in fact as Head he does not dispense grace without the instrumentality of the body he has joined indissolubly to himself. For those whom she cannot effectively reach by her proclamation, the Church prays, and offers the unbloody Sacrifice of the Altar, as well as the spiritual sacrifices of her own children, as carried out in union with Christ.

As if to reinforce the point that *Nostra aetate* must not be taken as a shutting down of the missionary shop, the second corpus of additional material which the *Catechism* would house under the heading of the catholicity of the Church is her missionary activity – here presented not, as is more customary, in connexion with the ecclesial mark of apostolicity, but as an inner necessity of the logic of catholicity. Texts from the Second Vatican Council are interleaved with quotations from Pope John Paul II's missiological encyclical, *Redemptoris missio*, to show how the Church cannot deny her missionary nature without repudiating her nature *tout court*: for mission is nothing but the communication, both as reality and as conscious reflection on reality, of the communion of the Trinitarian charity which graciously founds her own being and life. Such mission entails much hard work and sacrifice: it may involve poverty and persecution; it will always need patience; it can entail a concomitant ecumenical endeavour, for the bad example of divided Christians renders the Gospel less credible; it must always mean a respectful dialogue with those who do not yet believe.

The topic leads naturally enough into a discussion of the fourth ecclesial mark: the Church is not only one, holy, and catholic; she is also *apostolic*. She is founded on the witness of the apostles to the crucified and risen Lord; she preserves, assisted by the Spirit, the sound word of the apostolic preaching, and she continues to be taught, sanctified and governed by the apostles in the persons of their successors, the college of bishops under its Petrine head. The *Catechism's* treatment of apostolicity is dynamic – as must inevitably be, for the concept of apostleship is one of mandate for mission. The origin of all apostleship, all public representation, in the Church, is, as Jesus himself declares in St John's Gospel, the mission of *the* Apostle *par excellence*, the God–man, from the Father: 'As the Father has sent me, even so I send you' (John 20:21).

The perseverance of the Church in the apostolic tradition of faith and practice, as guarded by the succession of apostolic ministers, enables the revelation given definitively to the original apostles to be passed on by the whole Church, whether lay or ordained, in its integral purity and fullness. Apostolic faith and

Professing the Faith: The Creed on the Holy Spirit 129

order subserve, then, the wider apostolate of both clergy and laity: the diffusion of Christ's reign throughout the earth. Mention of the internal differentiations of the Church brings the *Catechism* to its *sixth* and penultimate ecclesiological approach, which lies in *the analysis of the various estates found within her body politic* – and notably three: hierarchy; laity; and those (chiefly Religious) who live the 'consecrated life'. The *Catechism* turns on its head the usual democratist objection to the distinctions of standing in the Catholic Church – the German for the technical term *ordo* which I have translated as 'estate' is, precisely, *Stand*. The differences between the Church's members are in function of the fuller unity and more effective missionary outreach of Christ's faithful. In this way the *Catechism* makes practical sense of the theological claim, in its preceding paragraph, that, by virtue of baptismal regeneration all the faithful have an equality of dignity in the body of Christ.

Since the whole Church is a sacred order – a 'hierarchy' – the *Catechism* must relate the place of the laity, her overwhelming majority, to that of ministerial priests (bishops and presbyters) and Religious in an integrated view. The ministerial priest does not owe his specific place in the Church to the common prophetic and royal priesthood based on Baptism but to the sacrament of Order whereby he is configured to Christ as Head of his Church *vis-à-vis* his mystical body, the community. Although the *Catechism* must postpone a full treatment of Order until it broaches its sacramentology, it makes certain salient points in this ecclesiological context. First, no one can become the sacramental representative of Christ the Head by their own decision. Only thanks to a mandate from the Church's Lord can bishop or presbyter proclaim the Word with doctrinal authority, lead the people of God in celebrating the sacraments of their salvation, and 'pastor' them by seeing to it that their community grows in the communion of charity which Church discipline exists to mould. No one by looking within their own breast can decide that they have a right to ordination – in the way sometimes suggested by the misplaced zeal of women avid for priesthood, chiefly in the Anglo-Saxon countries, nor can a community which has failed to put forward candidates with that *ensemble* of gifts the Church desiderates and yet simultaneously asserts a 'right' to the Eucharist, establish its own ministers. Avoiding polemics, the *Catechism* does not enter these debates, but by its serene presentation of the apostolic succession as a dominical sacrament given for the sake of the continuity of the apostolic tradition over time, it convicts of contempt those who speak slightingly of those so mandated as, overwhelmingly, a 'celibate male club'. Secondly, however, as if to offset any possible impression that the apostolic ministry is an élite possession, it insists on its character as *service.* Indeed, if priests effaced themselves more fully behind their objective work, and the ritual of the Liturgy, their bounden duty and service, rather than treating the first as an exercise of power and the second as a possibility for self-expression, there would be much less eagerness to conquer their office as a commanding height of the Church. Next, the *Catechism* underlines the collegial nature of Order: something which goes back to Jesus' selection of the Twelve. Considered as symbolising the whole people of God, the Twelve found the common priesthood of all the faithful, united as this is to Christ in his self-offering to the Father. Considered, however, as the original apostolic envoys of the Lord, the Twelve share in Christ's mission as Lord of his Church, sitting at the Father's hand, ever living to make intercession for us. Thus the Twelve are simultaneously the people of God and those sent into the world to form that people from the nations. Since their office is derived from the Twelve in this latter fashion, both bishops and presbyters must act senatorially, giving counsel to their fellow-ministers. However, the *Catechism* is at pains to balance this assertion with an affirmation of the irreplaceably personal quality of ecclesial office: each office-holder maintains his charge in the form proper to a disciple, namely, through personal responsibility to the personal Lord. Neither bishops not priests can take refuge behind bureaucracies and committees.

The holder of the Petrine see exemplifies the personal pole of the charge which is common to all the bishops, while the episcopate at large manifests the synodal or senatorial nature of that calling. It is, one may say, a leading difference of modern Eastern Orthodoxy from Catholicism that the synodal enjoys, at least in theory, a clear precedence over the personal. Although many Orthodox hierarchs show an alarming tendency towards the arbitrary in Church government, thanks to the unwieldy nature of a non-codified Oriental Church law, in principle Orthodoxy appears to have resolved the ancient tension between a gathering of bishops and its head in favour of the gathering, Catholicism in favour of the head. There cannot indeed be more than one ultimate subject of decision-making in the Church, one bearer of supreme authority. Although the ideal is a symbiosis of the conciliar and the primatial, in times of conflict within the episcopal college at large (including there the bishop of Rome), matters can only be resolved in one of two ways – either by the majority of a Council or by the pope. The Catholic Church has come historically, through a perception of the deficiencies of Conciliarism and the theological strengths of Ultramontanism, to find in the latter the key to the Redeemer's will for the governmental structure of his people. The papacy is not separate from the regular ministry which all bishops share, but it is unique in its mode of continuity and in the personal authority conferred by the charism of the papal office. The *Catechism* does not respond to the question, What then of bad popes? which comes so naturally to the lips of a generation more exercised at the past transgressions of institutions than by its own sins. Balthasar wrote:

> The Petrine office is both central and 'eccentric'. Certainly, this office was placed in the 'holy' centre of the Church (hence the demand for a declaration of love from the first pope). From this centre, however, it does not reach out only to the sinners who are displaced from it and thus 'eccentric'; it is not only *for* them but rather *with* them (it is Peter, who denied the Lord, who is given office), in such a way that the personal guilt of the office-holder does not vitally affect the indefectibility of the office. Peter is simultaneously though not in the same respect, *justus et peccator, fallibilis et infallibilis* ... This is the central 'scandal' of Catholicism that a sinner should claim an element of infallibility.[19a]

[19a]H. U. von Balthasar, *The Office of Peter and the Structure of the Church* (E.t. San Francisco 1986), p. 181.

Peter has to appear as an individual, and in this sense 'over against' others. He does this not by domineering, but as a servant who does not detach himself from either college or the wider ecclesial communion, but frees those who belong to each to be themselves in the true liberty of the fullness of the Gospel.

Under this universally primatial head, the bishops exercise a threefold office of teaching, sanctifying and governing. Here the *Catechism* faithfully reproduces the order of priorities given in *Lumen Gentium*, for, as the need for catechesis is not the least potent reason for affirming, the preaching of the Gospel – the teaching of the Catholic faith – is the indispensable foundation on which the bishop must build all else he does. Just because the pastoral office of the bishops aims at keeping their flocks in the liberating truth of Christ, their magisterium cannot be a mere 'pastoral magisterium' of exhortation, but must be a strictly doctrinal magisterium of dogmatic teaching, and hence a theological one at the same time. In reminding its readers of the intellectual duty to give one's adherence to the utterances of the teaching office – for even when what is involved is not in the fullest sense the 'obedience of faith', the 'ordinary' magisterium in its non-definitive exercise nevertheless proposes a fuller understanding of revelation and so warrants an allegiance connex with that obedience, the *Catechism* in no way implies that it suffices for pope and bishops to act merely preservatively, as guardians of inherited doctrine. By their prayers and labour, together with that of their presbyteral co-workers, the bishops are to sanctify their churches, not only through the ministry of the Word and sacraments but through their own example. The fervour with which a bishop prays for his diocese may account for more in its life than a materialist would think. Likewise, the sacred jurisdiction of the office-holder is not exercised in straightforward acts of legislative or executive authority alone, but comes through counsel, persuasion and, once again, example. Here the *Catechism*, in the wake of the Council, proposes the rudiments of a mirror for pastors – that *genre* beloved of the patristic and mediaeval Church: one remembers King Alfred's gift of 'his' translation of Gregory the Great's *Pastoral Rule* to the bishops of Anglo-Saxon England.

And yet it is the laity without whom the Church would look truly strange, and to them in their vocation at large, as well as in its participation in the threefold office of Christ, held in ecclesial fullness by the bishops, the *Catechism* now passes. The Church's Scriptures present the Christian people as a prophetic and royal priesthood, established by the Son, through the work of the Spirit, for the Father's glory – that is, for the realisation of his purpose. In distinguishing the lay faithful from Religious and the ordained ministers of the Church, the *Catechism*, in keeping, once again, with *Lumen Gentium*, stresses their rôle in redeeming the world of time, of matter and culture, of politics and work. Simultaneously, however, the laity are expected to be direct propagators of the Gospel, by evangelising, and being apostles of the faith, in their own environments – those parts which other Christians, whether pastors or Religious, cannot reach.

In speaking of the priestly office of the lay faithful the *Catechism* unifies all those multifarious activities – the directly and the indirectly salvific – by means of the concept of spiritual sacrifice. As a 'holy priesthood' they are to follow the apostle Peter's urging, and 'offer spiritual sacrifices acceptable to God through Jesus Christ' (I Peter 2:5), uniting them to that one Sacrifice which consummates all others, the Offering made by our eternal High Priest on the Cross and renewed sacramentally on the altars of the Church. Such consecration of the world has a privileged locus in the nurture of children, to whose parents Augustine ascribed an 'episcopal' office. Evangelisation can be considered as a priestly work inasmuch as it is a service to the Word of truth, for which, in Jesus' prayer on the night before he suffered, in the Johannine account, the apostles received priestly consecration. But it might more naturally be thought of under the heading of the prophetic office of the laity, which the *Catechism* now goes on to do. Contrary to what one might expect – the laity for doing, the pastors for speaking, the Religious for being – the book stresses the need for a laity articulate in all the media in which the Gospel can be pronounced. The witness that is one's life does not suffice; the world has need of words, though not of wordiness. The *Catechism* notes in particular the rôles of the laity in catechesis, in the sacred sciences (theology and its connected disciplines) and what in modern English we call, in debased fashion, 'the media'. (Church documents prefer, more correctly the phrase 'media of social communication'; a 'medium' must always be *of* something; its whole point is that it cannot stand on its own.) A final aspect of the prophetic function of laypeople in the Church is to speak frankly to their pastors about matters affecting the Church's good. In freely admitting this 'right' and even 'duty', the *Catechism*, and the Code of canons which it cites, draw attention to its pre-conditions – to be legitimate such criticism must be theologically well-informed, not impugn the totality of Catholic doctrine on faith and morals, show respect for Church office-holders, be ordered to the common good of the Church and not transgress the dignity of persons. (Not much doubt is left that many of the hectoring interventions which characterise a good deal of the contemporary Catholic press would fail to meet these criteria.) The regal office of the laity obliges them to carry out various, analogically related, kinds of 'ruling'. They are to master the disorder of sin in their own persons, and exercise their spiritual kingship for the good of others, spreading the spirit of the Gospel, expressed in Catholic values, to the society around them. Using their royal energies, the laity must seek to construct the foundations of a Christian civilisation, of which political ethics will form a necessary part. Though the Gospel is primarily concerned with things eternal, and transcends all sociology, nevertheless it gives us sovereign rules of conduct for life together, tracing a charter of behaviour to which any civilisation of Christian inspiration should conform, in ways dependent on the diverse conditions of history. The *Catechism* is right, however, to present ascetiscism as the first duty of the royal office. Otherwise what should be the fruit of love and personal generosity can degenerate into an egoistic enterprise forgetful of persons among our corporate neighbour – society.

It is a sign of the *Catechism*'s good sense that, in its presentation of the vocation of the royal and universal priesthood in these 'offices', it does not wish upon them a minute concern with the affairs of sacristy or deanery meeting. While gladly recognising the help lay ministers can give in 'extraordinary' circumstances when pastors are lacking for the breaking of the Word, and the administration of certain of the sacraments, and the contribution that a number of the faithful can make to the formulation of Church policy at different levels, only an introspective, nay claustrophobic ecclesiology could desire them to concentrate their redemptive resources on these inward workings of the household. The alternative vision, implicit in the *Catechism*'s account, is that the laity will use the charisms bestowed upon them to make of culture, in its widest sense and myriad manifestations, a theophanic point, from where God's glory shines out and converts the world by attracting it.

And so we come to that third estate of the Church, those living the consecrated life. Unlike the ordained minister, the Religious does not owe his or her specific place in the Church to a sacramental difference from the laity, but to their vocation to respond, by a special way of life, to the Holy Spirit as he brings to the Church some anticipation of the life of the Kingdom of God. The *Catechism* expresses this difference by speaking of *Religious* as embodying in a stable way of life recognised by the Church those evangelical counsels of poverty, chastity and obedience whose general spirit it is incumbent on all the faithful to manifest. The life which the Religious professes (its personal realisation is of course more variable) is wholly centred on God, in communion with their brothers and sisters, without giving or being given in marriage (chastity), and without self-definition by possessions (poverty) or by choosing one's own goals (obedience). Rooted as it is in the common gift of Baptism, it constitutes – as the *Catechism* emphasises, over against, in all probability, a more 'critical' concept of the difference being a Religious makes, a foretaste of the spiritual fruits of the Age to Come. If the distinction between lay person and ministerial priest lies in the differing rôles each plays in the economy of the Son, then the distinction between lay persons and Religious is founded on their different rôles in the economy of the Holy Spirit. The *Catechism* will return to this eschatology theme in the conclusion of its miniature theology of the Religious life. Meanwhile we can note here that these differences between priest, Religious and layperson, also render them complementary. Christ as Head typified by the ministerial priest, and the Holy Spirit who rests on Christ, typified by the Religious, need Christ's mystical Body, typified by the layperson, for the will of the Father to be made effective in the world.

A most important move is made when the *Catechism* initiates its more detailed survey of the phenomenon of Religious life in Catholicism by stressing the unity of that life as predetermined in its root. By using the metaphor of a tree with its branches, the *Catechism* tacitly presents all forms of Religious life as so many exfoliations from the monastic life which was, historically, its genesis. The insistence on the permanent validity of the monastic inspiration of all Religious life is essential to the maintenance of its fundamental norms and values – despite all the varied adaptations which a diversity of good works, and of spiritualities, legitimise and even demand. Certainly, the *Catechism* is not slow to recognise a wonderful plurality among the Orders, congregations and communities of Religious, something given fine expression by Stephen of Muret, founder of the erstwhile Order of Grandmont, when he wrote:

> In my Father's house there are many mansions, and there are many ways which lead to it. These various ways have been commended in writing by diverse of the Fathers and they are called the Rules of St Basil, St Augustine and St Benedict. These are not the sources of the Religious life but only its offshoots. They are not the root but the leaves. The rules from which all others derive, like streams flowing from a single source is the Holy Gospel[20]

– because there are paths of development ('trajectories') in the corpus of the New Testament literature which point onwards towards Christian monasticism, even while the idea of a distinctively consecrated life, among the various states of life in the Church, may come later.

The *Catechism* begins its account of the main individual forms of Religious life with that of the hermit. The eremitical

[20]Stephen of Muret, *Liber sententiarum*, prologue.

life appears first in the *Catechism* because it constitutes a sublime manifestation of the inner mystery of the Church – union, or, in warmer language, 'personal intimacy' – with Christ.[21] The Second Vatican Council had spoken of solitaries as following more closely the Christ who contemplated on the mountain, and seen their lifestyle as a secret source of fecundity for the Church. Pope John Paul II gave one hint as to how this might be when he wrote to the minister-general of Chartreux for the ninth centenary of the Carthusian hermits in 1984:

> The sons and daughters of the Church who are dedicated to apostolate in the world, at the mercy as they are of a perpetual mobility and evolution, need to rest in the stability of God and his love. This stability they contemplate palpably in you who have shared it more especially than the rest here below.

Given the pneumatological context of the *Catechism's* treatment of the Religious life (via ecclesiology), it is surprising that no echo is heard of St Thomas' strongly Spirit-oriented doctrine of the hermit life: for Aquinas, eremitism carries to an extreme pitch two of the essential means to perfection in Religious life (poverty and chastity), while the third, obedience, is radically altered. Actual obedience is no longer necessary: the solitary is led by the Holy Spirit. In its more christological vision, the *Catechism* sees the hermitage as a place of 'silent preaching', and the vocation of its occupant a call to spiritual warfare, finding in the desert (Tradition would say, for the sake of the city, the Church) the glory of the Lord whom the powers and dominations crucified.

Not that the solitary must necessarily live in the traditional 'desert' of lonely places, on sand, in woods, or mountains. The anonymity of life in a great city may do just as well. This is relevant to the second category treated here: that of the virgin, who may be either a nun, in some form of individualised cloister, or a woman living in the world. The state of consecrated virginity already glimpsed in Paul's Corinthian correspondence and the Johannine Apocalypse, is not only a living out of the

---

[21]Paragraph 921.

nuptial union of the Church with Christ (in which, as we have noted, the *Catechism* locates the Church's own mystery); it is also a state of life which allows of numerous possibilities for serving the Church: in rôles which vary with the Spirit's gifts from social worker to iconographer. The *Catechism* also envisages associations of such virgins on a diocesan basis, rather as in the *béguinages* of mediaeval Flanders.

And so we come to the coenobitic or communitarian Religious life, which the text is inclined to call Religious life *simpliciter*, the life in its limpidly classical form. A convenient *aide-mémoire* for its constituent elements is found in the Latin Code: it is a life which accentuates liturgical worship; it is characterised by the public profession of the evangelical counsels; it is a common life, a fraternal or sororal life, but it also has a vital inward, contemplative dimension which the *Catechism* signals by speaking of the testimony it gives to (once again) that sponsal relation of Christ to the Church which is the ecclesial mystery's heart. A plaudit from Pope John Paul II in his letter on mission records the missionary successes of monks and nuns, and this is surely owed not simply to their *disponibilité* but also to the fact that their communities, once created in mission lands, become at once micro-churches, miniature reflections of the whole life – at once worshipping, meditative and charitable – of the Church.

Two final groupings are more of a modern coda: the 'secular institutes' whose members, though of both sexes, are comparable with the diocesan virgins, yet, more specifyingly, work for the sanctification of the world (rather than the direct service of the Church), and the 'societies of apostolic life' which are, for the most part, coenobitic communities in the becoming, but where the common life is determined more fully than is usual by the demands of some special apostolic work. The *Catechism* does not enter upon the topic of the present condition of Religious life in the Catholic Church, which would be an undertaking outside the limitations of its *genre*. Should it do so, it might have to record that many once 'classical' communities now resemble more closely these last two types. Perhaps in the last analysis this does not matter greatly to the Church universal so long as the spirit of the Beatitudes – penitent, meek, peace-making, thirsty for righteousness, pure in heart – dwells in their midst. For these are the signs of the Kingdom *par excellence* in human living, as the monastic tradition – the sayings of the Desert Fathers, Cassian, Benedict – knows full well.

Here the *Catechism* would end its ecclesiology – except for a curious, though defensible, decision, which is to sub-introduce the succeeding clause of the Creed, on the *communio sanctorum*, the 'communion of saints', into the present discussion. This enables the makers of the *Catechism* to kill two birds with one stone. First, they are able to round off their series of ecclesiological approaches by a *seventh* – the number of fullness, that! – which would speak of the Church as *a communion both of holy gifts and among holy persons*. Secondly, by treating the latter – the communion of saints – as a tacit addendum to the clause on the holy Catholic Church, they are able to finish their entire ecclesiology at the same spot where the authors of *Lumen Gentium* laid their pens to rest: with the Blessed Virgin Mary, seen simultaneously as the crown of all the saints and type and Mother of the Church.

The justification of treating the *communio sanctorum* as tacit ecclesiology is found in the rhetorical question put by the fourth century Latin Father, Nicetas of Remesiana (in modern Serbia): 'What is the Church if not the assembly of all the saints?'[22] As the *Catechism*, and many of its sources, are well aware, however, the phrase *communio sanctorum* can bear not only a personal sense but an impersonal one as well. The Creed's commitment to a *communio sanctorum* is hard to interpret from an historical viewpoint. The ambiguity of the Latin – a communion of holy persons or in holy things? – allows for a reference here to the sacraments, and this is how much – but not all – of tradition has read it. A sermon on the Creed from the time of Charlemagne refers the clause to

> that holy communion, through the invocation of the Father, the Son and the Holy Spirit, in which all the faithful ought to participate every Lord's day.[23]

---

[22]Nicetas of Remesiana, *Explanatio Symboli*, sub loc.
[23]Cited by J. N. D. Kelly in *Early Christian Creeds* (London 1960²), p. 393.

Mediaeval theologians who took this line sometimes integrated the two possible genders of *sanctorum* by saying that the clause's object is 'the communion which the saints enjoyed', namely, the holy sacrament of the altar. In the eleventh century, Peter Abelard speaks of

> that communion by which the saints are made saints, and are confirmed in their sanctity, by participation in the divine sacrament.[24]

St Thomas, in his short commentary on the Creed, also tries to have the best of both worlds, remarking that:

> Because all the faithful form one body, the benefits belonging to one are communicated to the others. There is thus a sharing of benefits in the Church, and this is what we mean by *sanctorum communio*.[25]

Thomas explains that the 'goods shared' comprise everything worthwhile done on earth by the saints, but particularly the seven sacraments, since they alone convey to us the *virtus* – the power, or in the archaic English sense, the 'virtue', the peculiar property – of Christ's passion, the atoning act whereby Christ as Head redeemed his body, the Church. The sacraments are, in other words, a uniquely privileged sphere of the action of the Holy Spirit transmitting to us the reality (insofar as we can share it here and now) of the Son's redeeming work, that highpoint of the Father's love and mercy to the world.

The *Catechism* preserves the essentials of this approach – though its textual authority is not Latin at all but Byzantine, and specifically the words in which, in a number of the Eastern liturgies the celebrant shows the consecrated Gifts to the faithful prior to their communion. The acclamation 'Holy Gifts for those who are holy!' is beautifully interpreted in the *Catechism's* own pneumatological context, and missiological spirit:

> The faithful (*sancti*) are fed by Christ's holy body and

---

[24] Peter Abelard, *Expositio Symboli quod dicitur Apostolorum*, sub loc.
[25] Thomas Aquinas, *Expositio super Symbolo Apostolorum scilicet Credo in Deum*, sub loc.

blood (*sancta*) to grow in the communion (*koinônia*) of the Holy Spirit and to communicate it to the world.[26]

Atypical of the Western tradition is the decision to extend the impersonal sense of *communio sanctorum* way beyond the sacramental, and notably Eucharistic, gifts of God. The *Catechism* finds the 'communion in spiritual goods' to include, first and foremost, communion in faith – that apostolic treasure-hoard which, it remarks, grows the more it is shared, following the inverted monetarism of the Spirit. While, certainly, communion in the sacraments is mentioned next – and a fine quotation from the *Roman Catechism* draws attention to the special place here of the Eucharist, it is soon followed by communion in spiritual gifts, given, as First Corinthians has it (12:7) for the common good; communion in the riches of this world, of which individuals are but stewards; and communion in charity – where the *Catechism* puts forward, with assistance from Pauline thought, that notion of the spiritual repercussiveness of actions both good and evil which the Anglican lay-theologian Charles Williams described so profoundly under the name of 'the coinherence'.

Paralleling, and dependent on, the communion in holy things is the communion of holy persons, or, as the *Catechism* prefers to call it, 'the communion of the Church in heaven and on earth'. The single Church exists in three great phases: those who are making pilgrimage on earth; those who are undergoing purification, having passed from this life; and those who are enjoying the glory of seeing the Triune Lord of the Church, just as he is. This is the proper context for thinking of those two great hosts with whom we share the *koinônia* of the Holy Spirit in the holy Church: the saints, and those souls, not yet glorified, but departed in charity, whom Catholic piety, though conscious of their continuing need of purification still calls likewise '*the holy souls*'. In each case, the *Catechism* speaks both of the wider concept of communion with them, and the more specialised one of their intercession (or ours for them).

The cultus of the saints needs no commending to separated Eastern Christians, but it does so to Protestants, and to the

---

[26] Paragraph 948.

general enquirer. Its defence might well start with the question, Can the mediatory work of the Son made man – a work which, as the Letter to the Hebrews reminds us, goes on throughout time and eternity – itself be mediated? Can God by grace enable other human beings to share in Christ's mediatorial activity so as to become its channels to others? The Catholic view is that such sub-mediation is not only conceptually possible; it is a familiar feature of Christian experience. Examples would be: when people pray for each other 'through Christ our Lord', that is, in the power of his high priestly prayer before the Father; or when they take the Gospel to others, as agents or instruments of *the* Word of God, Jesus Christ. That Christ makes other human beings, the saints, into sub-mediators of salvation is a more powerful testimony to what we can call his salvific creativity than would be his simply saving us without any further sub-mediation of his atoning work. Few better ways to understand the cultus of the saints in Catholicism can be imagined than the graphic depiction of its rationale in the mediaeval Western rood screen. As Dr Eamon Duffy has written:

> The saints stood in the most literal sense under the Cross, and their presence on the screen spoke of their dependence on and mediation of the benefits of Christ's passion, and their role as intercessors for their clients not merely here and now but on the last day.[27]

The *Catechism* finds it impossible to improve on the statement of *Lumen Gentium*: the intimate union of the saints with Christ enables them to reinforce the holiness of the Church; they offer to the Father, by way of intercession for us, the merits they have acquired through Jesus Christ; our weakness is therefore much aided by their brotherly (and sisterly) concern. That many living saints, in the history of Christian hagiography, have seen things so is exemplified from the *dicta* of St Dominic (represented by the promise of post-mortem assistance immortalised in the Compline antiphon, *O spem miram*, in the Dominican use) and Thérèse of Lisieux (a more familiar

[27] E. Duffy, *The Stripping of the Altars. Traditional Religion in England, 1400–1580* (New Haven and London 1992), p. 158.

citation, in which, invoking the 'flower poetic' in vogue in French literature in her period, she promised to 'shower down roses', spending her heaven doing good on earth). The wider concept of communion with the saints in the *Catechism* is also indebted to *Lumen Gentium*, with its combination of the rationales of imitating exemplars and consolidating the union of the heavenly and earthly Churches by the cement of charity. For a fuller statement the reader – or catechist – might turn to the mediaeval Western text known as *Legenda aurea*, the 'Golden Legend'. In this work of the Dominican hagiologist James of Voragine, a sixfold rationale is offered by way of explanation of the cultus of the saints. First, that veneration gives honour to God, since whoever honours the saints necessarily honours as well the One who has sanctified them. Secondly, we venerate them so as to provide 'aid in our infirmity', so that we may deserve their assistance. Thirdly, in celebrating their glory, our hope is augmented. As Augustine remarked of the martyrs:

> They really loved this life, yet they weighed it up. They thought of how much they should love the things eternal if they were capable of such deep love for the things that pass away.[28]

Fourthly, we honour them so as to learn from their example. Fifthly, just as the saints rejoice in heaven over our repentance, so it is right that we 'make feast of them on earth'. Lastly, in worshipping them with the worship of devotion, we honour the whole communion of the Church 'for charity makes all to be common'. All personal salvational situations before God are reciprocally co-determined.

That being so, there must also be a place in Christian believing for communion with the souls in Purgatory too. To cultivate the memory of the departed has been treated as among the highest works of piety in Judaeo-Christianity since at least the time of the Maccabbees, 'When you're gone, you're gone' is not a maxim favoured by the Church, conscious as she is that the primordial dividing line in these matters follows a fault not in the biological continuum (between living and dead organisms) but in the christological continuum (between

[28] Augustine, *Sermon* 344.

those who are, and those are not, alive in Christ). And just as in the wider communion we enjoy with the saints, a special emphasis belongs with our petitions to them for their intercession, so too here: we can help the holy souls by our suffrages, just as their prayers, though they are our fellow-sinners, can help us on earth. This is a topic to which the *Catechism* will revert in its final chapter, on the 'life everlasting'.

Meanwhile it turns to the greatest of the saints, the Mother of God, but discussed now not in relation to the mysteries of her Son, or to the person of the Spirit of whom, as we have seen, she is the *chef d'oeuvre*, but as *Mother of the Church*. Three themes emerge: the spiritual motherhood of Mary; her specific cultus; and Mary as the Church's 'eschatological icon'. Singling out the Blessed Virgin from the circle of the other saints, whether canonised or not, and giving her so signal a place not only in devotion but also in soteriology, in an account of how the Church (not only earthly but heavenly) sub-mediates the redemptive work of Christ, is only defensible if Mary was herself joined in the closest fashion imaginable to the person and achievement of the Redeemer. It is in fact in Mary's co-suffering with the Victim of Calvary, her association with his sacrifice, and her loving consent to that dread salutary work that the *Catechism*, reproducing its ecclesiological charter, *Lumen Gentium*, founds its account of what the poet G. M. Hopkins calls her 'ghostly motherhood'. In saying 'Yes' to the Incarnation of the Son, Mary says 'Yes' to his redemptive work, and repeats that 'Yes' throughout his life, supremely so at the foot of the Cross where she is God's privileged *collaboratrix* in the New Covenant. Mary standing beside the Crucified is, *par excellence*, the Daughter of Zion on the great and terrible Day of the Lord. No wonder that Christians have sought to identify with the Mother of Sorrows. In the poetry of the eighth-century Irish writer Blathmac, the poet describes himself as seeking out Mary's company so that he may keen with her, and so come to share the quality of her response to the Word. If Catholic exegetes of all generations have found in the committal by Jesus of his beloved disciple to Mary as her son, and of his mother to John as his mother, an implicit declaration that the mother of the Messiah will be likewise mother to the messianic community (John 19:26–27), that event could have taken place, theologically speaking, at no other moment. Her perfect union with Christ in his self-emptying brings in its train a unique insertion into his redemptive triumph at its central point.

After the Virgin of Sorrows at the Cross, the *Catechism* counts as the second mystery in the manifestation of Mary's ecclesial motherhood her convocation with the disciples in the Upper Room, awaiting the descent of the Spirit – the Virgin of the Cenacle. Mary was thus present at the beginning of the Church, the start of the Church's pilgrimage through the history of individuals and peoples. It is the conviction of Tradition that her presence was not limited to that, but bestowed on the Church's entire journey through space and time, and notably as that journey is found in the history of souls – the microcosmic inner personal journey which accompanies and helps to compose the macrocosmic public and corporate journey of the Church.

Next comes the mystery of Mary's Assumption, which, as a mystery of hope, looks ahead to the *Catechism's* closing Mariological remarks on the Mother of Jesus as icon of the Church in glory. In the vision of the seer of Patmos in the Apocalypse, 'the Woman' represents the Church militant: she is the mother at once of the almighty messianic Child and of his brethren – in other words, of the total Christ, Head and members. But St John makes it patent that the woman is herself safe and sure, the worst that the enemy can do – sin and death, the 'powers of Hell' – has been powerless to take her in its thrall, though she remains one with those of her children who are still vulnerable to his attacks, in the warfare that continues on earth. Here we have *in nuce* the dogma of Mary's Assumption, which the *Catechism* treats as at once, and in its own prose, 'an anticipation of the resurrection of other Christians',[29] and also, in the troparion from the Byzantine office for the Dormition, or Falling-asleep of the Mother of God, a commencement of her powerful intercession. In her Dormition she did not abandon the world; on the contrary, having rejoined the

[29]Paragraph 966.

Fountain of Life, her prayers help free from death the souls of the faithful.

Mary is, then, not only the Church's model in faith and charity but the mother of Christians in the order of grace. In the work of salvation there are no privileges without responsibilities, no *noblesse* conferred that does not oblige, no sharing in the divine life which does not produce the most characteristic sign of that life – self-communication, self-bestowal. Mary's glorification is in one sense the end of her life, but in another sense its beginning. It is her entry upon her duties in the régime of transfiguration by which the world becomes the Church, sinful humanity the company of the redeemed, and the evil and mediocre turned into saints. At the Assumption, Mary initiates the activity prophesied by her dying Son when he gave her to the infant Church (represented in the last apostle) with the words, 'This is your mother' (John 19:27).

Because of the Assumption, we can call on Mary as not only Mother of God but also Mother of the Church, and call for her to exercise her motherhood with efficacy in our regard, asking that, through her, we may glimpse and be drawn toward the glory in which she is bathed, the radiance of the uncreated Love shining out in the face of the risen Son. Mary is called on, accordingly, as advocate, *auxiliatrix, adjutrix, mediatrix*, not so as to diminish the unique mediation of Christ but to show its power. For Christ's mediation flowers by stimulating participation in itself.

As a mediatrix – a facilitating intercessor – Mary's whole desire is that the messianic power of her Son shall be manifested. Always, as once at Cana, she presents herself as spokesman of her Son's will. This must be borne in mind when, in the fourth century, we hear St Ephrem call Mary the mediatrix, or in the ninth see St Tarasius of Constantinople salute her: 'Hail, mediatrix of all things which are under heaven, hail, reparation of the world', or in the twelfth century West find Bernard styling her 'the mediatrix to our Mediator', undoing Eve's evil mediation, the mediatrix who opens the bosom of mercy to all, so that no one can hide himself from her warmth. St Albert says that Mary was assumed by our Lord as a help in our salvation to be, like Eve for Adam, a 'helpmate like unto himself', communicating by privilege in his Passion. Thus the whole world is bound to God by the Passion of Christ, and, derivatively from this, to Mistress Mary by her compassion. We may echo an adage of Marian hyperdulia and say, *Nunquam satis de Maria*, 'one can never exaggerate the case for Mary' – but only if we are clear that in so saying what we are more fundamentally affirming is the superabundance of the redeeming grace of Jesus Christ.

And this is most relevant to the cultus of the Virgin, which now occupies the *Catechism's* attention. 'All generations shall call me blessed' is Mary's own prophecy in her Magnificat. The cultus of the Virgin is enormously varied in Catholicism. Its simplest form is a cry for assistance, as in the very early (possibly third century) prayer *Sub tuum praesidium*:

> We seek refuge under the protection of your mercies, O Mother of God; do not reject our supplication in need but save us from perdition, O you who alone are blessed.

But it can also take complex forms, as in the Rosary the 'Psalter of Mary', where prayers of acclamation and praise (the Our Father, the Hail Mary, the Glory be) are fused with meditation on the principal events of the lives of Jesus and Mary, the whole being presented via the mediaeval symbol of the rose – a garland of devotion for the Rose without thorn. Where mysticism is concerned, Mary's Rosary, warmly commended by the *Catechism*, is the people's charter. The Rosary puts the Gospel in a nutshell, and tells of how all can become contemplatives. The least sophisticated and most sophisticated can pray it in different ways, and by it all can become truly simple – looking to God with the prayer of simple regard, as Mary now sees him in her bliss.

Finally, Mary is the Church's eschatological icon: the sensuous representation, in space and time, of what heart cannot surmise nor mind conceive of that place beyond place and time out of time which God has prepared for those who love him. In the after-life, Mary reveals the Church's deepest aspirations, both in the new heavens, where it hopes to be re-united with Christ the Bridegroom, and in the new earth, where it hopes to hold sway in plenitude of spiritual power. But this power is made perfect in weakness, as St Bonaventure remarks of the Poor Man of Assisi's devotion to Mary:

He embraced the Mother of our Lord Jesus with indescribable love because, as he said, it was she who made the Lord of majesty our brother, and through her we found mercy.[30]

The final activities of the Spirit with which Creed and *Catechism* deal concern the raising up of man in all the dimensions which make him whole: the raising up of his soul through the *forgiveness of sins* (together with its extension in Purgatory, and its consummation in heaven); the raising up of his body through the *resurrection of the flesh*, and the raising up of his total spiritual and material environment in the transfiguration of the cosmos, the new heavens and the new earth, in *the life everlasting*.

The forgiveness of sins is, as Balthasar points out, a work of the entire Trinity.

'Father, forgive them', says the Son on the Cross. And the Father forgives because he sees how fully the Son forgives his debtors; and both pour the Spirit of Holiness into the sinner's icy heart so that it might melt and the love within it begin to flow.[31]

Yet this very quotation makes clear why the forgiveness of sins should be considered in a special way the mission of the Spirit, whom the risen Christ, in St John's equivalent of the Lucan Pentecost, breathes out on the disciples for this very purpose (John 20:22–23).

The *Catechism* does not propose to linger long on the subject in this context – even though, from one perspective, it constitutes the very aim of both Incarnation and Atonement. The reason for its haste is that, since the Spirit's forgiveness is embodied for Catholicism in the regenerative waters of Baptism, and in that re-actualisation of Baptism which is the sacrament of Penance, there will be time enough to contemplative it more leisurely in the future, when the sub-book on the holy sacraments opens. The *Catechism*, considered as a commentary on the

---

[30]Bonaventure, *Vita Maior*, IX. 3.
[31]H. U. von Balthasar, *Credo. Meditations on the Apostles' Creed* (E.t. New York and Edinburgh 1990), p. 90.

confession of faith, therefore, restricts itself at this juncture to a minimum statement. Baptism and Penance: these are its subject. It was the Lord himself who linked the hearing of the Gospel to the undergoing of Baptism, in the Great Commission at the end of St Matthew's Gospel: 'Go, therefore, and make disciples of all nations, baptising them in the name of the Father, and of the Son, and of the Holy Spirit' (Matthew 28:20). Baptism is that fundamental sacrament which enables us to receive the Word of God not as foreign to our nature but as the renewal of our true nature, now assumed into the ambit of the Life everlasting. It is the sacrament of that faith whereby, through the enlightening of the Holy Spirit, we respond to the Gospel of Christ, adhering to him and entering into the new Covenant he founded. For these reasons it must indeed be, as the *Catechism* says, the 'first and chief sacrament of forgiveness of sins':[32] without such forgiveness, without the overcoming of our most basic estrangement from God, the more positive aspects of baptismal transformation scarcely enter the picture. The *Catechism* presents Baptism as explicitly christological, implicitly pneumatological. As a celebration of the Paschal mystery, by which the barrier of sin is brought down and humankind reconciled to the Father, Baptism is a sharing in the mystery of Christ. It is the Good Friday of the individual believer. But in linking faith in the forgiveness of sins to faith in the economy of the Spirit in holy Church with its *communio sanctorum*, we are invited to approach this sacrament as initiation into life in the Spirit. Baptism is also the Easter of the individual believer, and there is no Easter without the Spirit who raised Jesus from the dead.

Although baptismal grace so edifies the powers of the soul that the Christian who co-operates faithfully therewith a whole life long may never sin, few there are so reckless as to claim such a spotless escutcheon. The *Catechism* recalls the rhetorical question posed by its Tridentine predecessor: Who has emerged totally unscathed from the spiritual warfare to which Baptism commits the Christian? And this is where the sacrament of 'second repentance' comes in: the baptised themselves need, alas, a sacrament of reconciliation with God and his Church.

[32]Paragraph 977.

We are to combine liberality towards the sinner with insistence that his or hers must be real repentance. Declaring roundly that there is 'no offence, however serious, that the Church cannot forgive', the *Catechism* explains that 'Christ who died for all men desires that in his Church the gates of forgiveness should always be open *to anyone who turns away from sin*'.[33] Penance as a Christian virtue, a permanent disposition to practice repentance of heart, is confirmed and brought to completion in this sacrament. Only by union with the Church, Christ's body, can the sinner re-find peace and the Holy Spirit. So Christian penance is only fully effective when sacramentally united with her. For this reason, the Church does not simply require the faithful to frequent this sacrament in the case of very grave post-baptismal sin – classically summed up in the unholy trinity of murder, adultery and apostasy. More than this, the regular submission of our wayward actions, words and even thoughts to sacramental penance consecrates our personal efforts at detachment from sin, and our struggle with the evil within and without.

The articles of the Creed on the resurrection of the flesh and the life everlasting are the culmination of the Church's profession of faith, for here, as the *Catechism* remarks, belief in Father, Son and Holy Spirit and their creative, saving and sanctifying activity soars to its climax in these stupendous declarations. That the flesh, despite or because of its weakness and mortality, will rise again (it is on what is most lowly that God chiefly delights to have pity), has been from earliest times not only an essential but a specifying feature of Christian faith. The *Catechism* cites to excellent effect Tertullian's ringing overture to his treatise on the destiny of the flesh: *Fiducia christianorum, resurrectio mortuorum.* The life everlasting experienced as the resurrection of the body – not simply for the individual but for the entire communion of the redeemed – is the ultimate Christian hope. In Christ there rose the whole reality of human nature, all that goes to make up its comeliness.

The *Catechism* traces the gradual revelation of this resurrection hope through the Scriptures of Israel. Such a

---

[33]Paragraph 982. Italics added.

hope represents, it suggests, the convergence of two motifs in the revealed religion of the Hebrew people. If God is the all-Creator, to whose work nothing – not even, for instance, the unformed matter which faced Plato's Demiurge, is anterior, then the whole human being is the object of his predilection. If, moreover, the covenant faithfulness he showed to Abraham and his seed is the adverbial style of all his activity, then will he not stay faithful to this creature of dust into whose nostrils he once breathed his life-giving Spirit? The surmise of the Maccabbees, Pharisees, and other groups in inter-testamental Judaism was confirmed by the Word made flesh who, moreover, bound the resurrection hope to the destiny of his own person in declaring himself 'the Resurrection and the Life' (John 11:25). When on Easter night, the Church celebrates the vindication of her Lord, and the confirmation of the truth of his message and saving work, she does not thank God simply for him but for herself too. Christ is the first-fruits of a wider harvest, the Head who draws the body with him to where he is. The Resurrection of Christ is both the seal on the Good News of the loving mercy of God (a theological truth in the strictest sense) and the promise of the transfiguration of human life and the cosmos where that life is set (and so a truth of anthropology and cosmology as well). To be a witness of his Resurrection was, the *Catechism* reminds its readers, *the* precondition for apostleship in the earliest Church (cf. Acts 1:22).

But how are the dead raised? The *Catechism* does not answer its own question save in the sense of identifying the ground of all possible answers: the almighty power of God, who wills, in his wise and loving plan for his creatures, to give them indestructible unity of body and soul, in dependence on the Resurrection of his Son made man. Suggesting as analogy the Eucharistic transformation, which is also a change of being in anticipation of the messianic banquet of the End of the ages, the *Catechism*, in harmony with Tradition, refuses to speak of the general resurrection except in connexion with that definitive resolution of history, both human and cosmic, which is the Second Coming. What Christ as Head exemplifies, his members are to become when he returns in the glorious

Parousia to shape our lowly bodies into the likeness of his lovely one. The salvation of the world, in the thinking of the *Catechism*, cannot prescind from the overturning of that separation of soul from body which mars the beauty of the human nature God made as a matter-spirit unity. Even now, through faith and the sacraments of faith, Christians begin to share this Resurrection life of the future, albeit in a hidden way. Dead and raised to life again in Baptism, prescribed the medicine of immortality which is the Eucharist, they carry this glory in non-manifest fashion within them. Hence, the *Catechism* concludes on a note of severe practicality, the peculiar urgency of Christian respect for the body, and above all for the bodies of those who suffer – in whom, by a kind of negative dialectic, the Resurrection life is most palpable. Resurrection is always for the dead, for those, like Lazarus, who are bound.

This link leads the *Catechism* to take as its next topic 'thanatology' – the theology of death, and more especially of dying 'in' Jesus Christ. It stresses the ambiguity of natural death. On the one hand, some inbuilt limit is necessary if our existence is to have a character of probation (there can be no meaningful test where the final tripos is indefinitely postponed). On the other hand, there is the disclosure of revelation that, while God made human nature mortal, he did not in fact intend it to perish. In that gracious design of his for our first parents, the intuitions of tragic art are confirmed. This waste was never 'absolutely' intended; it is but the permitted consequence of sin. The enigma of the positive and negative charges of death as humanity now knows it is resolved, for the *Catechism*, in the Passion of Christ, and notably in the Agony in the Garden. The obedient love, infinite in ramification, whereby the incarnate Son accepted death, though hating it, in a free submission to the Father's will, changed its meaning for ever.

Now, by what Hilaire Belloc called the 'chief miracle of the Incarnation' the phrase 'Christian death' is tantamount to the wishing of a blessing. Death is always painful, a fragmentation of our being, which God wished to spare us. But, in going before, Christ has made this way a redemptive one. If we follow him in trust, our death, while remaining painful, also becomes beautiful, a 'good death'. Ignatius of Antioch, on his way to martyrdom, hears a 'living water' within him murmur, 'Come to the Father'; the great Teresa, as usual telling it straight, wants to see God – but to see God one has to die; the little Teresa, in her *Novissima verba*, says most simply of all 'I am not dying, I am entering life'.

Here we have to do first and foremost, of course, with the Vision of God, to which the *Catechism* will shortly turn. But there is question also of a sort of 'telescoping' of the Christian hope, by reference to the primordial 'Christian experience' of Jesus himself. Just as the dying of the Lord was his letting-go into the hands of the Father, to awake again on the morning of the Resurrection, so the glorification of the soul, as through the Paschal mystery it enters the presence of God and the Lamb, is a definitive pledge of the resurrection of the whole human being: in Ignatius' words, 'Let me reach the pure light; once there I shall really be a man'.

The *Catechism* pleads for a recovery of the spirituality of *bona mors*, preparing for the hour of our death. Its decline in Western Catholicism, at least in the lands of the North Atlantic civilisation, with their sanitising reduction of dying to a clinical 'termination' of living, is one of the poisoned fruits handed to the Church by the world. The Litany of the Saints; the Hail Mary; and the traditional devotions to Joseph of Nazareth as patron of the good death, speak differently, as does St Francis' *Canticle of the Creatures*, with its amazing outburst, 'Praised be thee, my Lord, for our sister, Bodily Death'.

In moving from 'the resurrection of the flesh' to 'the life everlasting', the *Catechism* shows no immediate sign of changing the subject. Here too it opens on death, citing the magnificent Commendation of the Dying in the *Roman Ritual* – *Proficsere, anima christiana,* 'Go forth upon thy journey, Christian soul', to make the point that, while in one sense death is the moment when I am most utterly alone, in another sense I am then least alone, most suffused by the presence of the Church which draws life from the Passover of the dying Lord.

After death comes judgment: the 'particular' judgment which, in the *Catechism's* doctrine, sets out life in its true relation to Christ. The words of the Carmelite doctor John of the Cross, now quoted, do little more than repeat this assertion: 'At the evening of life, we shall be judged on our love'. Unlike Newman, who in the *Dream of Gerontius*, believing he was telling the supernatural story of the Church's Everyman, assumed that after judgment would come, for the 'normal' reader, Purgatory, the final purification, the *Catechism*, more optimistically, turns rather to consider the best of all outcomes of judgment: Heaven.

Those who die in the gracious friendship of God, and do so perfectly purified – that is, with their entire personalities transformed by justifying and sanctifying grace, will 'live forever with Christ' and 'see him as he is'.[34] The occurrence of the twin formulae is significant, because the *Catechism*, while anxious to maintain the traditional doctrine of the Latin Church, classically formulated by the fourteenth century pope Benedict XII, that Heaven consists in the face-to-vision of the divine Essence, also wants to do justice to the enduring mediatorial rôle of Christ's humanity in all human knowledge of God. The vision of God will be brought to us by the humanity of the Saviour, the Lord of the thorn-crowned head and the five wounds, the 'Lamb that was slain' whom St John presents as the central figure of the heavenly tableau (Apocalypse 5:6). By way of the sacrament of Jesus' glorified humanity, we come, in the Word, to share God's self-knowledge, being related to him as the Son is to the Father. In the Beatific Vision, the very Essence of God provides the form in which our minds may know his mystery – which otherwise infinitely exceeds them. Rather as, in everyday understanding, the concepts through which we know the world give the mind shape and structure, conforming it to the realities of things, so here, at the climax of our journey of understanding, we receive God himself as the structuring form of our intelligence. At the same time, our wills need divine strengthening too, if ever they are to be attuned to their almighty Object. Not the Light of Glory only but also the Fire of the Kingdom must set human powers ablaze: a fine text from St Cyprian's *Letters* shows the *Catechism* as sensitive on this point. And if the Catholic doctrine has been accused by the modern Eastern Orthodox of excessive cataphaticism, a note of apophatic restraint is added in the reminder that only by a profusion of images – light, life and peace; wedding banquet; wine of the

---

[34] Paragraph 1023.

Kingdom and house of the Father; paradise and heavenly Jerusalem – does Scripture attempt to speak of what eye has not seen nor ear heard, nor the heart of man given entrance here below (cf. I Corinthians 2:9). Comprehension and description alike fail at the thought of the blessed communion to be given both with God and with 'all who are in Christ'.[35]

For the *Catechism* does not neglect the 'social joys' of heaven. The Mother of the Saviour, the holy angels and the entire company of the blessed co-constitute the city of the redeemed. Indeed, in the loving Vision of God, who is the origin and goal of all reality that is not God, every other reality will be known and loved by the saints, in the manner and measure in which it concerns them. In their joyful understanding of the will and plan of the only God, they will enjoy a perfect gaze on the christological and pneumatological structure of redemption history – the universe in its irradiation by the energies of Son and Spirit, as the *Catechism* has so far described them.

It deals more briefly with Purgatory, the definitive purification of the soul, for which it retains the primary image, found in the Conciliar tradition, from Lyons II through Florence, to Trent, of a spiritual 'fire'. The fire of Purgatory is the burning presence of the love of God which an imperfectly purified soul cannot yet endure. Its sufferings are not only penal – though this aspect cannot be excluded, for effort is required from us for the undoing of a sinfulness which is freely forgiven by God but whose hold on us must nonetheless be cast aside. In contrasting the purgatorial fire so sharply with the condition of the damned, and presenting the inter-mediate state as essentially one of growth in holiness, the *Catechism* makes space for more therapeutic images. Purgatory is a period of healing for the still disordered psyche whose house the divine Charity needs time to put to rights. The Gaelic poetry of the Western Isles of Scotland sees Christ's people as purified there

> Till they are whiter than the swan of the songs,
> Till they are whiter than the seagull of the waves,
> Till they are whiter than the snow of the peaks,
> And whiter than the white love of the heroes.[36]

[35] Paragraph 1027.
[36] A. Carmichael, *Carmina Gadelica Hymns and Incantations* III (Edinburgh 1940), p. 371.

Rightly, the *Catechism* finds a major 'support' for the doctrine of Purgatory in the Church's practice of prayer for the departed. 'Remember, Lord', says the Roman Canon, 'those who have died and have gone before us marked with the sign of faith ... May these and all who sleep in Christ find in your presence, light, happiness and peace.' Though such prayers do not alter the eternal destiny of the dead, the intercession of the Church, united as she is to her Lord's sacrifice, above all in the Mass, causes them to benefit more fully from that sacrifice's fruits. The exiled archbishop of Constantinople, John Chrysostom, is, as the *Catechism* suggests by its choice of illustration, the doctor of this: It is because the economy of the Spirit embraces not only the forgiving of sins of those who await the resurrection of the flesh in the life everlasting but also the holy Catholic Church in the *communio sanctorum*, that confidence in Catholicism's ecclesial practice in these matters is well-founded. The giving of alms, the making of indulgenced prayers and actions, the carrying out of works of penance: these too are associated with that cultus of the faithful departed which is *par excellence* charity to the poor, for the holy dead are of all the poor the most deserving. The souls in St Thomas More's *Supplication* put it simply:

> Remember, friends, how nature and Christendom [that is, Baptism] bindeth you to remember us.[37]

Those ties are broken in Hell which is the occlusion of God as a consequence of the inward obduracy of man. As the *Catechism* puts it, 'We cannot be united with God unless we freely choose to love him'.[38] The lesson of Hell is not about the cruelty of God. It concerns the awful responsibility of human freedom, and the darkness and agony into which our daily acts may be insensibly leading us. In damnation a self-made judgment confirms the inherent outcome of a refusal to remain and grow in divine friendship. In the Parable of the Last Assize, the righteous, at their encounter with the Son of Man, go to a place intended for them, thus fulfilling their

---

[37] Thomas More, *The Suppliycacyon of Soulys against the Suppliycacyon of Beggars* (London 1529).
[38] Paragraph 1033.

destiny; the unrighteous go to a place never intended for human beings at all. The *Catechism* makes much use of that parable (Matthew 25:31–46), aware, doubtless, that its strongly marked social orientation – it is those careless of their neighbour's need who perish eternally – will win some sympathy for a hard doctrine. Of course, the Church has no authority to abandon doctrines deriving from the Lord, even when they are hard. And when all that can be said is said about the converting, paraenetic, existential and so rhetorical force of Jesus' sayings on Hell, it can scarcely be doubted that he held final impenitence to be a real possibility. It is indeed possible to lose the capacity for recognising justice and mercy, for seeing the truth. The Church, accordingly, forbids her ministers to preach universalism – the inevitable emptiness of Hell, just as she also forbids her members to arrogate to themselves divine judgment, and declare of any individual that they are reprobate. Far wiser is it to respect that unpredictable liberty of finite spirits which led St Paul at times to speak of all creation coming to a glad acknowledgment of God, at times to doubt his own salvation. Such respect for freedom mirrors God's own refusal to force the hand of creatures: as Dante placarded Hell in the *Inferno*, 'Love made me'.

The *Catechism* has already spoken of the general Judgment in its christological section, for it is the Son, on his return in glory, who is Judge of the quick and the dead. With the Lord's Parousia, this world will come to its end in universal judgment. if we ask what 'the world' is, the answer must be that it is the total set of relations of which we form part. The Church, making her own the voice of Scripture, prophesies that this total set of relations will come to an end, and a new set take its place. They will be such as to manifest the triumph of God's justice over the injustice of man, and, more than this, they will show how the divine love is stronger than death. By its allusion here to the Canticle of Canticles (8:6), the *Catechism* insinuates that the general Judgment will prove the history of the world to have been ultimately a love-song, though one filled with pathos, the divine wooing of a reckless race.

Its issue is the new heavens and new earth (II Peter 3:13) which constitutes the last word in Christian hope. The final and complete redemption of humanity is the general resurrection, for which, in Dante's *Paradiso*, even the blessed long. In its final citation of one of the main masters of its commentary on the Creed, Irenaeus, the *Catechism* speaks of the total ambience in which this *vita nuova* will be set: the visible universe itself will share in the glory of Christ. The Resurrection of the human body of the Son of God is in principle the glorification of the entire visible universe, the regeneration of the cosmos. The sacramental economy of the Church – which the *Catechism* will take as its next topic in a second book where we cannot now follow it – depends on this truth. Matter can be sanctified and sanctifying not only because, through the act of creation it is in itself good and beautiful and integral to human nature, but also because, through the Incarnation and bodily Resurrection of the Word, God has raised it to an incomparable grandeur and promised it an indestructible glory.

The final gathering-together of the universe can only be in Christ – in the perfect Image of the Father who represents not only the Father himself but all creatures, flowing as they do from that same Word. Inevitably, then, the cosmos, beautiful with creation's radiance, yet groaning with the travail of salvation, forms the wider 'temple' in which the Church's liturgy is celebrated – a point well made in the Welsh writer Saunders Lewis' poem 'Ascension Day'.

What's going on in the hills, this May morning?
Look at it all, the gold of the broom and laburnum,
The shoulders of the thorntree bright with its surplice,
The ready emerald of grass, the quiet calves;

The chestnut-trees have their candlesticks alight,
Hedgerows are kneeling, the birch is still as a nun,
The cuckoo's two notes over the hush of bright streams
And a ghost mist bending away from the meads' censer.

Before the rabbits scatter, O man, come forth
From your council houses, come and with the weasel

See the earth lift up an immaculate wafer
And the Father kiss the Son in the white dew.[39]

The Mass, which Lewis' poem takes as an anticipation of the redeemed world, ends its central prayer – the Canon – with the people's *Amen*. It is a little word easily overlooked by modern congregations. In the fifth century St Jerome describes it at this point in the Liturgy as ringing round the Roman basilicas like a thunder-clap: for then the *plebs sancta Dei* gave their glad assent to all the wonderful works of God, narrated by the celebrant over the *oblata* and turned by him into praise. The *Catechism* too makes much of the two syllables with which the Creed ends. Their Hebrew root denotes solidity, reliability, fidelity. The faithfulness of God is the ground of our confidence in him. His truth is trustworthy, his promises sure. It is, in the first instance, God himself, the *veritas prima*, who is the Amen, the ultimately credible One; the credo which gives the Creed its name is the human response to that. But in the second place, the daily life of Christians must be their Amen to the profession of faith they made, or had made for them, at their Baptism. We must be doers of the Word and not hearers only. But thirdly, and finally, the *Catechism* will have no self-salvation: such a mirroring of God's own faithfulness in personal existence is only possible through Jesus Christ our Lord, in whom all the Father's promises are 'Yes' – thus making him at once God's amen to man, and man's to God (cf. Apocalypse 3:14). In the words of the great Doxology, it is 'through him, with him, in him, in the unity of the Holy Spirit' that 'all glory and honour is yours, almighty Father, for ever and ever'. *Amen.*

---

[39]Translated from the Welsh original of S. Lewis, *Byd a Betws* (Aberyswyth 1941).

Index

I. Names

Abel 21
Abelard 139
Abraham 22, 27, 107, 151
Adam 46, 49, 50, 73, 74, 92
Afanas'ev, N. N. 117
Albert 146
Alexander, P. S. 69
Alfred 132
Ambrose 70
Anna 70, 109
Anselm 28
Aquinas, see Thomas Aquinas
Aristides 113
Arius 60
Athanasius 59
Augustine 18, 40, 43, 70, 78, 107, 118, 127, 143
Augustus 52

Balthasar, H. U. von 3, 68, 94, 114, 131, 148
Barth, K. 65
Basil the Great 28
Belloc, H. 152
Benedict XII 154
Benedict XV 60
Benedict of Nursia 139
Benson, R. H. 96
Bernard 63, 114, 146
Biasotto, R. P. 55
Blathmac 144
Bonaventure 39, 94, 147–148
Bosch, H. 46

Bossuet, J.-B. 76–77

Caesarius of Arles 34
Carmichael, A. 155
Cassian 139
Catherine of Siena 27, 43
Chareire, I. 46
Charlemagne 134
Chiari, A. 120
Clement of Alexandria 120
Clopas 64
Congar, Y. 24, 117
Cornelius 56
Cyprian 76, 120, 154
Cyril of Alexandria 60

Daniélou, J. 68, 106
Dante 157, 158
David 79, 107
Deutero-Isaiah 56, 85
Devlin, C. 89
Dominic 142
Duffy, E. 142
Duns Scotus 63

Elijah 78
Epiphanius 113
Ephrem 146
Eudes, J. 67
Eusebius 55
Eve 46, 50, 63

Fisher, J. 11
Foster, K. 120
Francis of Assisi 43, 147–148, 153

Index

Ghisalberti, F. 120
Gillet, L. 55
Goethe, J. W. von 93
Gregory the Great 132
Gregory Nazianzen 37
Gregory of Nyssa 59, 91
Guardini, R. 111

Hague, R. 88
Hegel, G. F. W. 40, 101
Hermas 113
Herod the Great 52
Herod Antipas 75
Hopkins, G. M. 88–89, 144

Ignatius of Antioch 124–125, 152, 153
Irenaeus 20, 30, 56, 59, 63, 74, 100, 104, 118, 158
Isaiah 34, 56, 70, 89
Israel (Jacob) 22

James, apostle viii, 64
James of Voragine 143
Jansenius 49
Jerome 159
Jenson, R. W. 35
Jezebel 78
Job 21
Joan of Arc 55
John, apostle 8, 27, 50, 54, 58, 59, 71, 82, 87, 128, 145, 148, 154
John the Baptist 50, 56, 67, 68, 108
John XXIII 1
John Paul II 1–8, 13, 15, 53, 115, 126, 128, 137, 138
John Chrysostom 110, 156
John of the Cross 153–154
Jones, D. 87
Joseph 56, 64, 153
Julian of Norwich 41

Justin 64, 113

Kelly, J. N. D. 139
Kereszty, R. 52

Lactantius 38
Lazarus 152
Leo the Great 53, 70, 116
Léthel, F.-M. 88
Lewis, S. 158–159
Lossky, V. 108
Lubac, H. de 115, 117
Luke 23, 64, 85
Luther, M. 49

Manzoni, A. 115
Mark 10, 5, 85
Marmion, C. 66–67
Mary, Blessed Virgin see Subject Index
Mary Magdalene 95
Matthew 5, 10, 58, 64, 79, 85
Maximus the Confessor 48, 88
Maximus of Turin 63
Moses 22, 78
McDade, J. 83
McPartlan, P. 117

Newman, J. H. 48, 154
Nicetas of Remesiana 139
Noah 21
Noujelm, G.-P. 28

Origen 54, 64, 76

Paul, apostle 11, 17, 18, 38, 49, 51, 63, 89, 93, 95, 103, 107, 110, 118, 137, 157
Paul VI 4, 71, 125
Paul of Samosata 60
Paulinus of Nola 89–90
Peter, apostle 7, 34, 55, 56, 77, 78, 115, 121, 131, 132, 133

Peter Chrysologus 63
Pfaff, R. W. 55
Pius V 5, 15
Pius IX 63
Pius XII 62, 126
Plato 151
Pontius Pilate 52

Rastell, W. 11
Ratzinger, J. 3, 26, 30, 117
Reynolds, E. E. 11
Romanos the Melodist 68

Sade, D. A. F. de 49
Saint-Exupéry, A. de 45
Schweitzer, A. 87
Scotus, see Duns Scotus
Second Isaiah, see Deutero-Isaiah
Stephen of Muret 136
Symeon 70, 109
Tarasius of Constantinople 146
Teresa of Avila 153
Tertullian 150
Thérèse of Lisieux 123, 142
Thomas Aquinas 14, 19, 20, 28, 59, 64, 78, 105, 123, 137, 139
Thomas More 156
Thurian, M. 8
Tiberius 52
Toynbee, A. 40
Tuckett, C. M. 69

Vergil 67

Weinandy, T. 53
Wiles, M. 53
Williams, C. 141
Wright, N. T. 69

Zechariah 56
Zizioulas, J. 117

II. Subjects

aesthetics, theological 1
angelology 41–42
apostolic preaching 23–24
apostolic succession 24
apostolicity *see* Church

Baptism 148–149, 152

Catechesi tradendae 12, 53
catechesis, importance of 12
Catechism of the Catholic Church
  and adaptation 7, 14–15
  aims 4–5, 7–8, 12–13
  Christocentricity 7
  and mission 10–11
  origin and development 2–4
  sources 4–5, 13
  structure 5–6, 13–14, 111
Catechism of Christian Doctrine (Penny Catechism) 123
catholicity *see* Church
Christ
  and Adam, *see below, under* titles
  Ascension 95
  Baptism 72–73
  burial 91
  conception and birth 58, 62–65
  death 84–89
    and Eucharist 87–88
    as sacrifice 84–85, 87–89
    and Trinity 88–89
  Descent into Hell 91–92
  human and divine knowledge 61–62
  Incarnation 59–61
  infancy and hidden life 67–72
  and Jewish opposition 80–82
  journey to Jerusalem 79
  and Kingdom of God 75–76, 77
  mission 104–105

Resurrection 92–95, 151
return to judgment 96–97
Session at the Right Hand of
  the Father 95–96
Temptations 47, 74–75
titles
  Adam, Second or Last 49,
    50, 65, 74, 89
  Christ 55–57
  Jesus 54–55
  Lord 57–58
  Son of God 57
  Son of Man 56
  Suffering Servant 56, 85–86
Transfiguration 77–78
trial 82–83
Church
  apostolicity 128–129
  catholicity 76, 124–128
  as communion of holy gifts 139–
    –141
  as educator 30
  estates
    bishops 132
    laity 129, 133–135
    Petrine office 77, 130–132
    Religious life 129, 135–139
  and Eucharist 117–118
  holiness 103, 115, 122–123
  and Judaism 126
  and life of Jesus' disciples 76–77
  marks 120–129
  and Mary 72, 115, 123, 139,
    144–148
  and mission (*see also* apostolicity)
    109–111
  as mother 29–30
  as mystery or sacrament 44,
    111, 114–116
  names and symbols 112–113
  and non-Christian religions
    126–127
  office 116–117

  and Order 129–130
  Passion of 96–97
  in plan of God 113–114
  and the poor 76–77
  and sacraments 115
  as Temple of Holy Spirit 118
  and Trinity 116–120
  unity 120–122
communio sanctorum see saints,
  communion of
covenant 21–23
creation 38–40, 42–43
Creed, Apostles' 5, 6, 13, 30–31
Creed, of Nicaea-Constantinople
  27, 30

death 48–49, 152–153
Dei Verbum 23–24, 25

earth, new 157–159
eschatology 109–110
Eucharist 87–88, 117–118, 152
Evangelii nuntiandi 12, 125
evil, problem of 37–38, 40–41, 47

faith 17, 25, 26–31
  ecclesial 29–30
  personal 27–29
Fall *see* man

Gaudium et Spes 120
General Catechetical Directory 12
God
  existence 18–19
  as Father 33–34
  immanence and transcendence
    35, 40
  known through events 20–23
  omnipotence 37–38
  participation in 48
  speaking about 19–20

Hail Mary 55

Heaven 153, 154–155, 157–159
Hell 156–157
holiness *see* Church
Holy Spirit
  and the Church 103–104, 109, 111
  in last times 104
  and mission 103–105, 109–111
  and sacraments 103
  and saints 103
  and Scripture 102, 104, 105–106
  in time before Christ 104, 106–108
  in time of Christ 104, 108–109
  and Tradition 102–103

irreligion 18

judgment 96–97, 153–154, 157

Kingdom, keys of 77
Kingdom of God 75–76, 77
knowledge
  of Christ 51–53
  of God 20–23

life everlasting 148, 150, 153
Lumen Gentium 112–114, 116, 124, 126, 132, 133, 139, 142–143, 144

magisterium 4, 13, 24–25
man
  body and soul 44
  Fall of 46–50
  as image of God 40, 43–44
  male and female 44–46
Mary, Blessed Virgin 56, 58, 155
  Annunciation 62, 63–64
  as archetype of faith 28
  Assumption 145–146
  and Church 72, 115, 123, 139, 144–148

  and Circumcision of Jesus 69, 70
  and Eve 50
  Immaculate Conception 62–63
  as our Lady of Sorrows 71
  and the 'poor of the Lord' (*anawim*) 23, 108
  virginity 64–65
  mission 10–11, 103–105, 109–111, 128–129
mystery, Christian 5–6

Nostra aetate 127–128

On Some Aspects of the Church as Communion 125
original sin *see* sin

Penance 148–149, 150
Pentecost 109–111
prayer and spirituality 5, 6, 14, 111
Providence 35, 40–41
Purgatory 143, 148, 154, 155–156

Redemptoris Mater 126
Redemptoris missio 128
resurrection 148, 150–152, 158–159
  of Christ 92–95, 151
revelation 17–26

Sabbath rest 43, 91
sacraments 103, 111, 115
sacrifice, Christ as 84–85, 87–89
saints 4–5, 103
  communion of 123, 139–144, 149, 156
Satan 47
Scripture 24–26, 102, 104, 105–106
sin 46–49
  original 38, 49–50

sins, forgiveness of 148, 149

Ten Commandments 5, 6, 14, 111
theodicy *see* evil, problem of
Tradition 4–5, 24–25, 102–103
Trinity 6, 31, 34–37
  and Church 116–120
  and death of Christ 88–89

Unitatis redintegratio 120–122
unity *see* Church

Vatican II (*see also individual Documents*) 1–2, 4, 12, 44
Vision of God *see* Heaven

www.ingramcontent.com/pod-product-compliance
Lightning Source LLC
Chambersburg PA
CBHW062002180426
43198CB00036B/2141